The Complete Guide to

Finesse

Bass Fishing

by Michael Jones

The Complete Guide to Finesse Bass Fishing
Copyright © 1991 by Michael Jones

Published by
McGRADY MEDIA
31566 Railroad Canyon Road
Suite 707
Canyon Lake, Calif. 92587

Cover photograph by the author.

Printed in the United States of America

ISBN Number 0-9630200-0-5

About the Author

Growing up in Southern California, Michael Jones opted for fishing tackle, not surfboards, and eventually turned his angling hobby into a full-time profession. As fishing editor for *Western Outdoor News*, Jones began experimenting with finesse tactics - and writing about them - in the early 1980s. Later, he expanded his writing and photographic horizons with work for a variety of fishing publications including *BassMaster®* and *B.A.S.S®. Times*.

In addition to his journalistic endeavors, Jones also serves as a consultant to several national fishing tackle companies. And, he is the creator of the popular *Pro League Bass™ trading cards*.

Jones lives with his wife, Clarissa, in Canyon Lake, California.

About the Artist

The bass pencil sketch featured on several pages was created exclusively for this book by the internationally-known wildlife artist and former All-Pro punter for the Los Angeles Rams, Dave Chapple. Chapple's original etchings, paintings and bronzes are in constant demand by private collectors, corporations and galleries.

Acknowledgements

The one person on this planet who shares most all of my memories about the "early days" of finesse fishing, who saw what I saw, learned what I learned and then tried to convince the rest of the fishing world that finesse really worked is my good friend and colleague, George Kramer. In George, I was fortunate enough to find a great fishing partner and an even better friend.

At roughly the same time, I was fortunate to forge another lasting friendship with Al Kalin, who believed in the power of finesse and in making lures that really worked. In Al, I found a man who embodies two of the attributes I respect most: honesty and the best, pure wingshooting ability I've ever seen.

I would like to extend a special thanks in the production of this book to the pros who shared their expertise with me. Thanks to Ken Cook, Rick Clunn, Shaw Grigsby, Guido Hibdon, Greg Hines, Larry Hopper, Don Iovino, Gary Klein, Rich Tauber, Joe Thomas and Don Siefert.

An extra special thank you to Gary Klein, who has lent me his support in this and other endeavors over the years. In addition to being a truly great bass fisherman, Gary has developed equally admirable skills at being a friend.

And, to my friend from Chicago, Paul Prorok. Thanks for tempering my western outlook with your midwestern roots.

Table of Contents

To Clarissa,
for always believing.

To my parents,
for giving me everything I needed
to be what I wanted to be.

Splitshotting

The Myths

If there is a truly misunderstood bass tactic, splitshotting is it. For reasons I don't quite understand, a number myths about splitshotting have been fostered by bass fishermen who have little or no experience with the technique and certainly even less success.

Much of this misinformation centers on several key fallacies:
- Splitshotting is slow. *It's not*
- Splitshotting only catches small fish. *It doesn't*
- Splitshotting will not win tournaments. *It will.*

The key to effective splitshotting is recognizing that this tactic is unique. Yes, it has a passing resemblance to a Carolina rig. And, yes, you fish it on spinning tackle and light line like many other finesse baits. But, in the final analysis, splitshotting is splitshotting is splitshotting.

The Method

Quite simply, splitshotting is a horizontal, moving-bait technique used when bass are moving through or holding in water 20 feet or less. While some anglers do splitshot at depths greater than 20 feet, I have found this depth range to mark the point of diminishing returns for the splitshotter. Excessive line bow, slow sink rate, tough strike detection and inaccurate targeting of casts make splitshotting less efficient beyond 20 feet while making vertical techniques such as doodling or darter jigging much more productive alternatives.

By duplicating the natural, swimming motion of a baitfish with the slow, steady retrieve of a small 4-inch worm, splitshotting is a very efficient means of force-feeding unaggressive bass. In most cases, this is accomplished by Texas rigging a 4-inch curl-tail worm on a straight-shank, perfect bend Aberdeen style hook with a splitshot crimped 18 to 24 inches up on 6-pound test line. The Aberdeen hook is used because it provides a keel to the worm which, like a boat's keel, keeps the worm on a straight and level course.

The Movement

Contrary to popular opinion, the worm does not have to float well off the bottom for a splitshot rig to be effective. Actually, the worm moves rather close to the bottom with its tail fluttering delicately and looking very much like that baitfish we're trying to mimic.

Although some fishermen place a splitshot on their line and call it splitshotting, the essence of the technique is in the moving bait tactic. Without the movement, you are merely placing a plastic worm in the water with a weight up the line. While this method does work, particularly with reapers, it is more an example of fishing *with a splitshot* than splitshotting. Also, it is an exceptionally slow method that only offers one advantage of splitshotting - the weight separated from the lure.

Since the proper retrieve maintains constant bottom contact with the splitshot while moving the bait at a slow, but steady pace, splitshotting covers water faster than just about any conventional worming method. Actually, splitshotting more closely resembles crankbait fishing than it does plastic worming. And, as a result, this method is especially lethal at locating fish concentrations or intercepting bass as they move up during daily migrations.

> *Maintaining constant bottom contact with the splitshot while cranking at a slow, steady pace is the key to splitshotting success.*

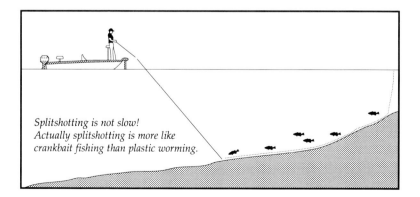

Splitshotting is not slow!
Actually splitshotting is more like
crankbait fishing than plastic worming.

The Advantages

As one becomes more adept at splitshotting and supremely confident in its ability to produce bass under any circumstances, one fiendish realization is this: You're not fishing for the same fish as everyone else. Correctly evaluated, a textbook splitshotting situation will yield bass only on a splitshot rig. Or, such an overwhelming number that using anything else just doesn't make sense. But, if bass can be taken consistently on some other lures, say crankbaits, then you have made a mistake in choosing the finesse approach.

While it is unfair to label splitshotting as a desperation ploy, the technique is clearly designed for tough conditions or for locating bass concentrations in large flats or along stretches of barren shoreline. However, in its pure finesse form, splitshotting can add productive hours to your fishing day by giving you an option on difficult days or during those inevitable "down" periods of otherwise good days. Instead of simply pounding away with the same lure during slow periods, splitshotting offers a viable alternative that not only adds bass to your livewell, but something more important — confidence.

If there is one pure joy from splitshotting (other than absolute confidence) it is in the ability to pull fish from so-called "used water." And, from unattractive areas that have remained unfished for years.

Long, sloping points, main lake flats, mud banks, swim beaches, launch ramps and sandy shoals are just some of the nondescript areas that attract bass yet deter bass fishermen. Occasionally the crankbait or topwater fishermen will roll through these areas, quickly casting here and there for a reaction strike, but mostly these zones are left undisturbed.

When fellow outdoor writer, George Kramer and I were investigating and refining the splitshot method in the early 1980s, we were amazed at the bass populations which frequented these forgotten areas. And, this was in the heavily-fished waters of Southern California where discovering pristine water is like finding a Mercedes Benz without a car phone.

Splitshotting Water

Of course, we quickly recognized that the very same precepts for good bass fishing structure related just as strongly to splitshotting water as it did to more traditional bass fishing areas. The difference is this: splitshotting water often doesn't look as good when its covered with water. But, if you could drain the lake and evaluate splitshot country, there would be all of the prerequisites needed for attracting and holding fish — migration routes, access to deeper water, forage, cover, etc. — as one would find in areas littered with more visual clues.

> *To find productive splitshot water, you need to retrain your thinking. Look for more subtle areas that hold fish, yet cannot be fished effectively with conventional methods.*

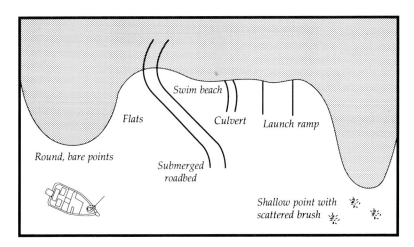

Swim beach

Flats

Culvert

Launch ramp

Round, bare points

Submerged roadbed

Shallow point with scattered brush

With experience, the skilled splitshotter recognizes the subtle elements of what makes for good water and evaluates splitshot areas just as he would with any other lure or technique. In each area, there are more productive zones that will hold and concentrate fish better than others. In splitshot water, what holds fish is simply more subtle. As a result, you have to re-tune your critical eye and evaluate the area based on splitshotting requirements.

Working with the Wind

Wind is the bane of every worm fisherman. Not only does a breeze make casting and bottom contact more difficult, but it greatly hampers strike detection. Generally, when the wind picks up, most worm fishermen opt for a crankbait or other lure than can be worked effectively on wind-blown banks.

Since splitshotting is a moving bait technique, wind can actually work in your favor. In the first place, windy conditions push most worm fishermen away from downwind shorelines, flats and points. Once again, a splitshotter is not fishing for the same fish as everyone else.

Second, wind action can push baitfish up into splitshot areas and trigger the feeding instinct in roaming bass.

*Size up in splitshot
and shorten the splitshot-to-hook distance
in windy conditions.*

However, even in splitshotting, some adjustments must be made when faced with windy conditions. In addition to sizing up in splitshot size, the splitshotter needs to adjust the distance from splitshot to lure. It should be remembered that the 18- to 24-inch distance is but a guideline. This distance can be shortened to 12 inches in windy conditions to reduce the amount of line bow between weight and lure.

Fortunately, splitshot bass hold onto the bait much longer than with normal Texas-rig setups. So, even with downwind casts and correct technique, strike detection can be the result of seeing your line moving three or four feet to one side. In these situations, simply reel up the slack and deliver the normal splitshotting sweep set.

Despite the built-in limitations in using light line and finesse gear, splitshotting does balance things out, especially in windy weather, by giving you a much greater margin for error in detecting strikes. Use it to your advantage.

When to Splitshot

• *Tough bites* - There are a number of tipoffs to the right time for splitshotting with the most obvious being a lack of strikes. In the right hands, a splitshot rig nearly guarantees a fish or two on any but the most dismal fishing day.

But, even more important is the ability to assess those times when the fish seem marginally active, but unwilling to hit with much gusto. Short strikes on conventional, Texas-rigged plastics, fish that follow fast lures like crankbaits and spinnerbaits but will not strike and shallow bass that spook easily are some of the common problems solved by splitshotting.

> *Splitshotting is very capable of producing quick limits from your worst water.*

Remember, IF THE FISH WILL HIT SOMETHING ELSE AS OFTEN AS A SPLITSHOTTED BAIT, YOU DON'T NEED TO SPLITSHOT. Unfortunately, those moments when you have to generate one lousy strike are far more frequent than when you have to decide which lure will produce more strikes.

For tournament situations, splitshotting is very capable of producing quick limits out of your worst water thereby saving better water for later on. Also, it is a very effective means of getting that final, limit-filling fish out of an area when the bass have been worn out seeing your spinner or crankbait.

• *New water* — Unless you have some excellent, up-to-the-minute fishing information about a new lake, the process of eliminating water can be a time-consuming one. And, it can be haphazard.

After all, if you work an area throroughly with a spinnerbait, all you've proven is the bass in that zone won't hit a spinnerbait. With splitshotting, you can be fairly confident that any fish with an ounce of aggression in him will take a swipe at a splitshotted bait. Of even greater value, with splitshotting, you can get a handle on the relative feeding tempo of the bass and apply that knowledge to which other lures and which other areas should be tried.

Of course, splitshotting will serve no benefit as a fish locator if you ignore the prevailing conditions or seasonal pattern. In other words, when the fish are holding in 25 feet of water on the edge of creek channels, dragging a splitshot rig around in 6 feet of water will not produce very impressive results.

With the help of your electronics, first determine the depth where most of the activity (both bass and baitfish) occurs. Then, to limit your search, choose the most optimum splitshotting areas — main-lake flats, sloping points, secondary points, submerged roadbeds and the like — to focus your efforts. By doing so, you should be able to develop a reasonably accurate picture of the fish concentrations in any unfamiliar lake.

Determine the key, fish-holding depth, then fish parallel to keep your bait in the strike zone longer.

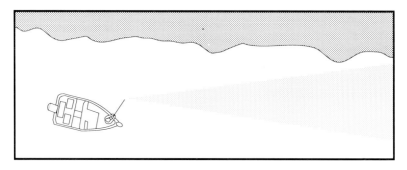

• *Dealing with changes* — Changes in weather and water are generally the most disconcerting factors for bass fishermen, especially for those bassers who cannot pick and choose which days they can go fishing. A sudden cold front, dropping water levels or temperature, boat traffic, fishing pressure or any number of other adverse conditions often force fishermen into completely revising their gameplans on the water.

Whether these environmental factors simply move the fish into different areas or push them into neutral or negative feeding modes, splitshotting is one of the best finesse methods available to locate, re-locate or simply prod mulish bass into biting when everything else appears to have turned against you.

Evaluating Splitshot Water

• *Re-train your thinking* - At first, it may be difficult to re-train your thinking as to what constitutes good bass water. In splitshotting, you're searching for more bland, "nothing" looking areas that hold fish, but have remained effectively untapped because no one has been able to find a productive way to fish them. Or, even bothered to unlock their potential.

• *By traditional standards, splitshot areas usually don't look good* - While "textbook" splitshot areas may appear uninteresting from above the water, rest assured there are reasons below the surface for bass being present. Granted, this may be secondary water on the bass housing scale and it may hold fish in scattered populations, but they do hold fish. And, these areas hold substantial numbers of bass because of their sheer size (huge flats, long stretches of shoreline) and because the fish have been pushed out of other areas due to environmental factors, boat traffic or fishing pressure.

• *Take in the big picture* - Once you've chosen a promising area, such as long, apparently uneventful, stretch of shoreline, sit back and take in the big picture. Somewhere along that shore there will be a small cut, a broken down fenceline or merely a change from mud to scattered rock. Use these visual clues to begin your sonar search.

• *Migration routes may be subtle* - With the help of your electronics, you're looking for the migration routes which bass can use to move up along this shoreline or whatever area you're investigating. Occasionally, you will be surprised by some very obvious structure, cover or breaklines that lead the bass to the shallows. Unfortunately, these underwater thoroughfares are generally the exception, not the rule, when it comes to genuine splitshot water. Normally, the routes by which bass move up into these less obvious areas are much more subtle - being marked by a gentle change in the bottom contour and posted with only a few, scattered stickups or rockpiles. The point? If the structure was that obvious, the bass concentration would be enhanced, more traditional worming methods would be effective and, most likely, every good bass fishermen in three counties would have wet a line here.

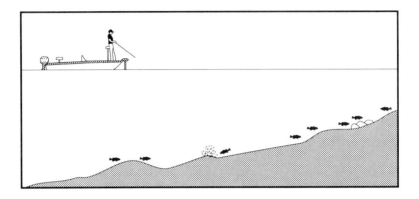

In good splitshotting water, the routes by which bass move up are much more subtle - being marked by a gentle change in the bottom contour and posted with only a few, scattered stickups or rockpiles.

• *Limit your search with electronics* - While splitshotting is a very effective means of locating fish, do yourself a favor and limit your search by identifying the most productive depth with your electronics. If it is possible to pinpoint that depth range, then parallel casts to the shoreline will keep the bait in the strike zone longer.

In splitshotting, you're searching for more bland, "nothing" looking water.

But, if the bass are scattered over a broad depth range, splitshotting is especially effective in covering ground. By fan casting in a manner similar to crankbait fishing, you can cover a large point, flat or shoreline much more quickly than with any other worm fishing method. Once again, this is why splitshotting is generally a MOVING BAIT TECHNIQUE, NOT A PULL-AND-JUMP METHOD. By maintaining constant bottom contact with the splitshot and moving the bait at a slow, but steady pace, you can present a splitshot worm in a very natural way, even in strong wind or current conditions.

Proper Presentations

• *Going out* - By definition, a bolo cast with a splitshot rig will never approach the fluid artistry of an underhand pitch with a spinnerbait. With the splitshot located anywhere from 12 to 20 inches from the lure, the splitshot rig is obviously lacking in esthetics and grace. But, with just a little practice, your accuracy can become rather dependable.

Through years of trial-and-error, I've settled on basically two casting styles: either straight overhead or a looping sidearm delivery. In both cases, the bait is suspended at reel height and the casting motion is a very deliberate one to avoid any sharp jerking or snapping of the line, splitshot and lure.

• *Coming back* - In splitshotting, there are two basic types of retrieve (other than drifting or moving with the trolling motor):

(1) A straight and steady, slow crank with the splitshot maintaining constant bottom contact.

(2) With the tip pointed at the water, the rod is swept back slowly while maintaining bottom contact. Once the sweeping motion is complete - and without allowing undue slack in the line - the excess line is reeled up while smoothly moving the rod tip forward. Then, the rod is swept back again and the motion repeated.

In both types of retrieve, the rodtip should be pointed at the water to maintain optimum rod control for hooksetting. (See Hooksetting, page 20)

Strike Identification

Although some strikes will come on the fall, the overwhelming majority occur while the lure is being retrieved. And, of these, over 90 percent will be "pressure bites."

A "pressure bite" is best described as a dull, mushy sensation that makes your bait feel as if it is snagged on a wet paper bag. Although it sounds difficult to imagine, experienced finesse fishermen can recognize these subtle hits as quickly as a topwater slam on a Zara Spook. **Perhaps the best way to familiarize you with this sensation - other than an actual strike - is this simple exercise: Place a rubber band over your thumb and index finger. Then, close your eyes and slowly stretch the rubber band back-and forth between your two fingers.**

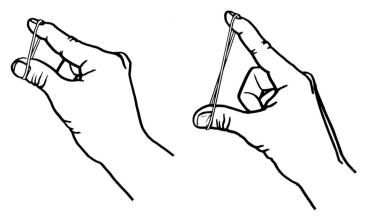

When learning the feel of a pressure bite under actual fishing situations, the best rule of thumb is to set the hook when anything feels out of the ordinary. While this may result in some snags and lost gear, the alternative - missed fish - is not a particularly appealing one either.

Even veteran splitshotters should follow this advice since stickups and sparse cover often mask bonafide strikes and, by the time you have determined that the pressure is actually a bass, it will be too late.

Fortunately, most splitshot fish will hold onto the small, unweighted worm or grub like a police dog on a cat burglar.

The Strikes

• *The Follow* - In this instance, the bass sees the bait and follows it until its aggressiveness or curiosity initiates a strike. In some cases, the bass will simply stop the lure. In others, it stops the bait and then moves off.

• *The Ambush* - This strike is usually in or around cover where the bass are holding. Again, the bass will simply stop the bait and hold it there. This is precisely why pressure bites occurring around cover are more difficult to detect. After pulling your splitshot and bait through countless small snags, it often becomes a guessing game as to which is the real thing. The ambush-oriented bass tends to let go of the splitshotted lure more often than any other. For that reason, ambush pressure bites can become a real guessing game in actual fishing situations.

• *The Surprise* - Although the splitshot bumping along the bottom and stirring up mud is not generally a key factor in generating strikes, it can be - especially when bass are very spooky or tenative. Under these circumstances, the bass sometimes focus on the silt kicked up by the splitshot and cautiously follow the weight, not the lure. Then, when they loose interest and stop following the splitshot, the lure suddenly appears nearby triggering a reaction strike. While this type of strike seems to be less common, it definitely comes in to play when fishing for visible bass in shallow, clear water conditions.

Hooksetting

Since the basic approach of splitshotting - a moving bait fished on light tackle - is very different from most traditional, Texas-rig tactics, an equally unique style of hooksetting is required.

• *The sweep set* - Instead of reeling down and rearing back (as is the case in Texas-rig hooksets), the hooksetting method used in splitshotting is simply a smooth and firm sweep of the rod. With your rod pointed at the water during the retrieve, the sweep set is merely a very deliberate movement of the rod to one side. If you keep the line "tight" while reeling during the strike detection phase - right through the sweep set - the sweeping motion is normally not an exaggerated movement.

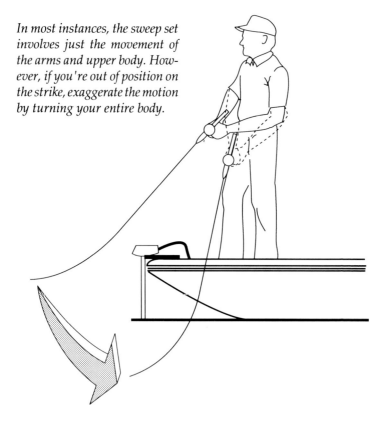

In most instances, the sweep set involves just the movement of the arms and upper body. However, if you're out of position on the strike, exaggerate the motion by turning your entire body.

Hooksetting continued

• *Rod position* - Rod position during the retrieve is critical since the low position of the rodtip (pointed at the water) makes for a much smoother, sweeping motion. If the rod is held too high, there is a greater tendency for a sharp, upward swing - a move that can either cause the line to break or, more commonly, the hook to bend before it imbeds in the bass' mouth.

• *Loading the rodtip* - One good habit to develop in hooksetting - and one that actually aids in strike detection - is to gently load up the rodtip as you feel pressure. Then, simply extend this motion while increasing the pressure. Remember, the needle-like, thin-wire hooks used in splitshotting generally set themselves once you start reeling and moving the rod. Especially since fish often hold the bait firmly while moving off in a direction away from your line of pull.

• *When the fish comes at you* - In those instances where the fish actually moves towards you, the pressure from the initial strike seems to come and go. Then, the it becomes a race between how fast you can reel and sweep versus how fast the fish is moving towards you. Often, this is the time when you must exaggerate the sweep of the rod by turning your body away from the fish and reeling fast.

Backreeling

While advancements in fishing tackle have come a long way since the cane pole days, there is still nothing more sensitive in the fish-to-fisherman connection than the human hand. When presenting a lure to bass, we depend on the sensitivity in our hands to feather the line during casts, detect subtle strikes and forcefully set the hook. Unfortunately, after the strike occurs, fishermen find themselves at the mercy of mechanical systems that depend on drag washers to insure that large or particularly hard-fighting bass stay on the line.

In finesse applications, light-line and small hooks narrow the margin for error dramatically - even when a caring angler takes care of the basics like premium line, strong knots and sharp hooks. One method which shifts the percentages in favor of the fisherman, but is routinely ignored even by professionals is the backreeling tactic.

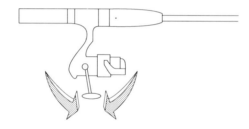

If you're already familiar with backreeling and don't like to do it, you might groan at the very mention of the word. But, if there is one technique crucial to avoiding breakoffs with light line, this is it. Quite frankly, if you refuse to backreel, you are placing yourself in the legions of splitshotters who worry about breakoffs. Assuming that you frequently check for line abrasion, retie often and keep bass from sawing themselves off over rocks rocks or cover, VERY FEW FISH ARE LOST WHEN BACK-REELING.

Although many novice finesse fishermen concern themselves with the effects of a crimped splitshot, breakoffs due to splitshot are vastly overstated. In fact, most of the trouble for finesse fishermen is the result of depending on a mechanical system to do what your own two hands can do a thousand times better.

Backreeling continued

• *How to do it* - Instead of depending on the drag to release line, the angler disengages the anti-reverse mechanism (which allows the reel handle to turn both forward and backwards) and gives or takes line during the fight by reeling forwards or backwards. To account for sudden bursts from the bass, the drag mechanism is set slightly higher than normal, but light enough to give line without a breakoff. With the drag set correctly, a backreeling angler should be able to control most fish without the drag coming into play.

Should a fish move too fast, simply open the palm of your reel hand and allow the reel handle to lightly brush your palm.

Often, the first reaction from fishermen not familiar with back-reeling is "How can I possibly reel quick enough to keep up with a fast-moving fish?" This is a common misconception. Actually, there are very few times when a bass moves fast - or far enough - to outpace the line-giving capability of a spinning reel. And, the more you backreel, the more you learn to anticipate just what a bass will do. However, should a fish move too fast, you simply open the palm of your reel hand and allow the reel handle to lightly brush your palm to prevent an overrun. When the bass ends its run, grab the handle and continue the fight.

• *Battling big bass* - In fighting large fish, backreeling is especially helpful since the line is not being taxed by the friction of a drag system. However, big fish (and many hot-fighting smaller bass) will make runs faster than your hand can move. In these situations, slightly cup the palm of your off hand and lightly touch the spinning handle to keep the reel from backlashing.

While most "big-fish stories" incorporate some recollection of 50-yard runs, this is generally pure fantasy. Actually, most large fish chug away very deliberately and head for deep water. What backreeling offers in both big and small fish situations is a very measurable degree of control. With drag systems, you are at the mercy of mere hardware - hardware that you may or may not have set properly in the first place. With backreeling, you depend on the sensitivity of your hands, hands which can be trained through practice to provide the best drag system any-where. And, this training should take place on every fish you catch - from subkeeper to limit maker.

> *With drag systems, you are at the mercy of mere hardware.*
> *With backreeling, you depend on the sensitivity of your hands.*

• *Forcing fish* - If you have limited experience with light-line and thin wire hooks, you will quickly learn that finesse fishing demands a good dose of patience in fighting fish. In fact, once the bass top the keeper-class size, forcing a fish to the boat clearly is not an option. Instead, your only choice is in how well you control the fish, let him tire and then get him in the boat.

Since the majority of splitshotting is done in areas of sparse cover, there is generally very little need to force the fish out of or away from certain spots. Of course, this rule becomes more flexible in direct proportion to the size of the bass hooked. Obviously, if a fish is heading for trouble, you need to make some very calculated decisions on how much you can pressure this fish without losing it.

• *Handling fish close to the boat* - The most direct benefit from patiently, yet deliberately fighting a splitshot bass comes when the fish is next to the boat. If you've tired the fish adequately (without unnecessarily extending the fight), the bass should come to the boat pretty much whipped.

When the fish tires and comes close to the boat, you can then switch the anti-reverse lever back on to leave one hand free for lipping or netting. It's a simple technique that many fishermen could benefit from if they invested a little time in learning - learning which can best be accomplished on smaller bass in non-pressure, non-tournament conditions.

Tackle

With the growing popularity of splitshotting, there has developed an ever widening chasm of misinformation about this technique. And, nowhere has this been more apparent than in the tackle items merely tagged with the "splitshot" moniker and foisted upon an unsuspecting populus. While some of these products do deserve your attention, a far greater number seem to be nothing more than the end product of someone out to make a fast buck on an emerging trend.

While I am certainly not the final word on splitshotting tackle, the following suggestions are based on years of trial-and-error under a variety of fishing situations from coast to coast. Quite simply, there are some things that work better than others. Much better.

I firmly believe in the theory often expressed by such great bass fishermen as Rick Clunn and Gary Klein that every lure or tactic is a tool. And, like the tools in a mechanic's toolbox, lures also have their very specific uses.

In finesse fishing, you just can't be what I call a "sledgehammer mechanic." The very nature of this subtle discipline of bass fishing demands using only those things which have proven themselves to be most effective. By ignoring this credo, you will simply be accepting mediocrity with open arms.

Rods

• *Length* - While the optimum rod length for splitshotting varies from brand to brand, there is a very recognizable point of diminishing returns. Generally, this point is reached when the rod approaches the six foot mark.

At this point, the tip section becomes far too responsive and begins telegraphing a confusing set of signals to the fisherman. Yes, you want a highly sensitive rod, but not one that reacts to every minute pebble and twig as the splitshot skims along the bottom.

Generally, a rod in the 5'3" to 5'9" range is the optimum rod over the broadest range of fishing conditions

Not only can the tip of a long rod send too much information to the angler, it can actually mask genuine pressure bites by taking too long to "load up." Instead of feeling the fish an instant after the pickup, the fish may actually be moving off with the bait before a strike is detected. Now, instead of a smooth and straight sweep set, you'll find yourself reeling up slack to find a bass that may have already made a left turn around a stickup. If it's a small fish, you may come out on top. If not, it's usually *adios*. And, if you're fishing in wind or current situations where you're already dealing with some slack line, a super-sensitive tip section only compounds the problem.

Generally, a rod in the 5'3" to 5'9" range is the optimum rod over the broadest range of fishing conditions. Not only does the tip section offer the proper blend of responsiveness and sensitivity, but the shorter rod becomes a real blessing when working bass close to the boat. And, remember, the standard splitshotting retrieve is done with the rodtip pointed at the water - a factor which can make longer rods more awkward. Of course, there are times when a good six-footer offers certain advantages, especially when longer casts are required.

Rods continued

• *Action* - Before we get too far along in this discussion of rods, one thing should be made very clear: Baitcasting gear just doesn't cut it in splitshotting. Aside from the obvious limitations in casting control, the balance and retrieve speed capabilites of baitcasting gear certainly do not offer any advantages over spinning tackle.

In choosing the proper rod action, you must start with the word "medium" printed on the rod. Then, you'll have to compare this somewhat relative designation with other medium actions of other brands to see where it fits on the stiffness scale. While you may start feeling like Lazarus looking for the last honest man, there are medium action rods out there that do not lean too much either to the heavy or light side of the equation.

And, there are some medium/light actions which can do the job quite nicely. However, they are more a rarity than a rule. The point is this: Don't buy a rod just because someone says it is a finesse rod. Pick it up, look it over and, above all else, compare.

• *Handle design* - There are no hard, fast rules in selecting a handle for splitshotting other than absolute, total comfort. Since you'll be working this rod slowly and smoothly, the onus is really on which handle design suits your fishing style.

One serious drawback, however, is in a rod handle that is too long. If you saddle yourself with a long handled rod, you'll quickly discover the error of your ways. The rod handle will forever be catching on your clothing and often be a hindrance when sweeping the rod during hooksets.

Reels

• *The simpler, the better* - While reel designers are constantly trying to come up with new features to catch our attention, most of them are of little benefit in a splitshotting reel. Forget fighting drags and all manner of extraneous knobs or gizmos. If you ascribe to the backreeling technique, you won't need them anyway and, with six-pound line, you'll soon appreciate the lack of anything that can serve as a snag.

• *Drag systems* - Mechanically, the venerable front-drag reels are more efficient than rear-drag setups, but there is a definite convenience factor with the rear drag systems. Whichever you choose, the overriding consideration should be one of smoothness.

> *Forget all manner of extraneous knobs and gizmos.*
> *Most new features are of very little use on a splitshotting reel.*

• *Anti-reverse levers* - For backreeling, the position of the anti-reverse lever is rather important and should be positioned on the reel in absolutely the most convenient spot possible. A raised lever or angled switch that you can find simply by feel is generally superior to a flat, push-type switch. If possible, avoid those reels with three-position switches that feature a middle, spool centering stop. While the spool centering feature is handy when making casts, it only confuses the issue when backreeling.

• *Size* - Clearly, a well-balanced splitshot rig will pay back huge dividends in efficiency, but don't push the balance thing too far. While a splitshot reel should be small and light, some tiny reels have equally tiny spools. The smaller the spool, the less line per crank can be retrieved and the more coils must come off the spool during a cast.

Again, there is a point of diminishing returns as you downsize in reels. So, stop at that size which gives the best ratio of spool size to reel size.

Line

If you've read more than one issue of any bass fishing magazine, there would seem to be very little reason to expound on the virtues of using high-quality, premium fishing line. Yet, there are some who ignore these warnings or, worse, do not change their premium line often enough to ensure that the most critical link between fish and fisherman is dependable.

With the lighter 6 and 8-pound test lines commonly used in finesse fishing, it is not only imperative to maintain the quality of your line, but to make sure that everything which contacts the line - from bail rollers to line guides - are absolutely free of any imperfections that can spell disaster.

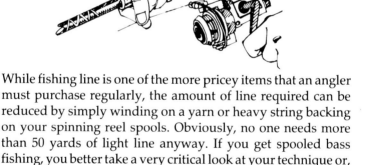

While fishing line is one of the more pricey items that an angler must purchase regularly, the amount of line required can be reduced by simply winding on a yarn or heavy string backing on your spinning reel spools. Obviously, no one needs more than 50 yards of light line anyway. If you get spooled bass fishing, you better take a very critical look at your technique or, more than likely, you've hooked a very large catfish or striper.

• *Line qualities* - Regardless of the brand name, the attributes necessary in a top splitshotting line are low stretch and maximum sensitivity. However, even with the latest technology, compromises must be made between these two elements to build fishing line that doesn't tip the scale too far in either direction.

With thin-wire hooks and light line, some shock absorbing stretch is necessary to avoid overwhelming these delicate ingredients. But, push the stretch factor too far and you handcuff yourself with a marked decrease in sensitivity.

Line continued

• *Coated lines* - Although the new, coated lines add greatly to the abrasion resistance and castability of a fishing line, they are not suitable for splitshotting applications. Unfortunately, these outer coatings prevent the splitshot from maintaining a solid grip on the line and cause the weight to slide down with very light resistance.

• *Spooling line* - Many of the hassles associated with throwing light line are preventable since most are self-inflicted. If a spinning reel is spooled improperly - with the coils reeled on against their natural grain - you'll spend a most frustrating day on the water battling a seemingly endless array of snarls.

A simple formula to remember when spooling line is this: The line must come off the factory spool in the same direction the reel turns. Unfortunately, not every reel cranks in the same direction.

When spooling a spinning reel, always lay the line spool flat on the ground. Don't put a pencil through the middle and wind it on as you would with a baitcasting rig. Then, crank the reel approximately ten times and check for kinks. If you lower the line towards the ground and the line twists, you're putting the coils on backwards. Simply turn the factory line spool over and try again. The line between spool and reel should fall in gentle coils.

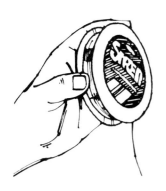

WRONG

RIGHT

Splitshot

While describing the characteristics of a splitshot may seem as enlightening as a discourse on the dynamics of a dirt clod, there are some important differences.

• *Round splitshot* - When removable splitshot was invented, I'm sure many expected the demise of the traditional, round shot to follow shortly. Unfortunately, the very feature that makes removable splitshot so handy - those protruding "ears" - also make them snags waiting for a place to happen.

No matter what brand of splitshot you choose, it must be round. Common sense will tell you that round shot can be pulled across most bottom contours with a minimum of resistance.

• *Softness* - A simple test for gauging proper softness is this: If you can squeeze the splitshot closed by hand, then you're in the ballpark. This means that the force required to firmly attach the shot to your line with pliers will be minimal and cause less flattening of the line.

However, if the splitshot is too soft and distorts when pressure is applied, you no longer have the snag-resistant, round shape required. Often, these overly soft splitshot will distort simply by rattling together in your tacklebox.

If you're fortunate to have a local tackle shop that stocks splitshot regularly, consider it a blessing. Most tackle stores, even those in splitshotting havens, are not geared up for the serious finesse fisherman. Generally, once you find a splitshot brand that works well, splurge a little and buy a good supply. The same advice goes for any finesse terminal tackle.

The No-Split Shot Solution
Greg Hines' Super Stopper

When fishing a rocky or uneven bottom, a 1/16- or 1/8-ounce slip sinker can be substituted for the splitshot by using an inventive snubbing method developed by Arizona pro, Greg Hines. With just a rubber band and a piece of monofilament, Hines' "Super Stopper" makes the slip sinker a viable alternative to the splitshot.

But, while this rigging method is handy, the slip sinker does subtlety change the dynamics of the splitshotting presentation with regard to how the lure moves through cover or across structure. If you switch to the "Super Stopper" because it proves to be more productive in certain situations, that's fine. But, if you're using this rig to avoid the splitshot, think again. The splitshot is not a major cause of breakoffs. Leave that to poor technique.

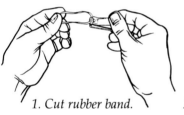
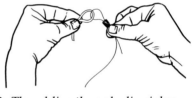

1. Cut rubber band.

2. Thread line through slip sinker, through rubber band, then back through sinker.

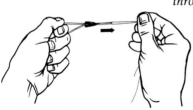

3. Using the line, pull the rubber band through the slip sinker.

4. To use, pull rubber band taut, then simply insert line through slip sinker. The distance to the lure can then be readjusted as required without crimping the line.

Hooks

• *The Aberdeen hook* - Without question, splitshotting has given new life to a forgotten hook style, the straight-shank, symmetrical (perfect bend) Aberdeen hook. This is the mainstay of the splitshotter's arsenal.

While the "perfect bend" and thinner wire of the Aberdeen style is inherently less strong than the heavier wire, asymmetrical Sproat, used in most conventional worming techniques, there are other advantages to the Aberdeen that far outweigh hook strength.

Since splitshotting is a moving-bait tactic, the straight shank of the Aberdeen serves as keel to keep the curl-tail worm or grub upright in a natural, swimming motion motion. And, it provides a straight pull during hooksets that keeps the hookpoint driving forward in the same direction as the bait.

As helpful as the bent-shank worm hooks (designed to turn in a fish's mouth) may be in other bass fishing disciplines, they are not recommended for splitshotting. This is because splitshotted worms need a keel for proper action - a requirement that is counteracted by the twisting motion built into this special breed of worm hook.

• *Hook sizes* - In most cases, a No. 1 Aberdeen will be your standard size for the majority of 4-inch, splitshot worms. For worms with somewhat thicker bodies, size up to a 1/0. For smaller lures, such as reapers, a No. 2 is recommended.

Over the years, those brands which have proven themselves in the splitshotting trenches are Mustad's No. 3263 Aberdeen and VMC's No. 9146. Another worthy addition to the finesse arsenal is Gary Klein's Black Weapon hook. Although the Weapon sports a shorter shank, it does offer a highly effective, rounded point for needle-like penetration and a stronger, Sheffield steel, Aberdeen-like design.

When splitshotting grubs, size up one step further with the Weapon hook to the 2/0 size which is clearly the best choice when splitshotting thick-bodied grubs.

Hooks continued

Pictured are VMC Aberdeen No. 9146 hooks (from left sizes 2, 1 and 1/0)

Texas rigging, Finesse style

Despite a few, offbeat rigging methods that have emerged here and there, only Texas rigging results in a properly keeled, splitshot bait.

IN ORDER TO PUT AS MUCH OF THE HOOK BELOW THE WORM FOR KEELING PURPOSES, YOU SHOULD TAKE A MUCH SMALLER "BITE" WHEN INSERTING THE HOOK THROUGH THE TOP OF THE WORM. While this tends to rip the worm more often on a strike, it effectively puts more of the hook where you want it.

Great care should also be taken to use the "seam" of the worm as a guide when Texas rigging. This "seam" is the result of injection molding and gives you an exact reference point where to bring the hookpoint through at the top of the worm and where to re-insert the point through the body. Properly done, the finished product should be absolutely straight on the hook without any subtle kinks or bends.

Although handpour worm specialists may wince, the flat side created when hand pouring worms tends to create a more unbalanced lure with greater tendencies to "roll over" during the retrieve. While handpours certainly have their place in finesse fishing, injection-molded lures generally deliver better keeling results.

Since Aberdeen hooks do not normally offer any bait-holding barbs, a splitshotter can prevent the worm from slipping down the hook by leaving a small tag end of the line at the knot to help hold the plastic worm, which is pushed up past the hook eye to cover the knot.

Splitshotting Lures

• *The 4-inch, curl-tail worm* - Despite the protestations of lure manufacturers who do not make a 4-inch, curl-tail worm, there is no one splitshotting bait that can beat this design for overall effectiveness and versatility.

However, not all 4-inch worms are created equal. The crucial difference comes in their relative abilities to produce maximum action at minimum speeds. Among bass fishermen, tail design in plastic baits seems to be a much misunderstood topic. While thinness of the tail is a plus, it does not alone ensure proper action. To a much greater degree, the design of the tail - the subtle relationship of the inner and outer curves of a tail design and how the tail converts forward speed into action - plays a more important role. Obviously, any lure that combines thinness with proper design will be a winner.

A GOOD TEST FOR ANY SPLITSHOT BAIT IS QUITE SIMPLE: IF THE LURE CANNOT GENERATE MAXIMUM ACTION (AT SLOW SPEED) IN THE LENGTH OF A SMALL AQUARIUM, FIND SOMETHING ELSE TO USE.

Splitshotting Lures continued

• *Grubs* - If there is one way to upgrade in fish size, the grub is it. With its bulky body and more pronounced tail action, the grub has proven its ability to attract larger bass.

With more plastic for the hook to penetrate, you should always upgrade your hook size to a larger 2/0 hook and consider moving up a notch in line test from 6-pound to 8-pound test.

If there is any drawback to the grub, it is in the very thing that makes it so effective: tail action. Again, this goes back to proper design since a grub that requires too much speed to work effectively can produce enough torque to overwhelm the splitshot rig and roll over. Similarly, if you're retrieve speed is too fast, the same roll-over situation can result. If either condition is present - a poorly designed grub or a fast retrieve - the twist in your line will unhappily alert you to the problem.

• *Reapers* - Splitshotting has elevated the leech-like, reaper-style bait to a popularity never previously attained by this pedestrian little lure. The rise of the reaper is probably due in large part to the fact that many splitshotters began slowing their retrieves to a near crawl during extremely tough bites and discovered that the do-nothing look of the delicate reaper-style plastics offered an irresistible tidbit for especially unaggressive fish.

Perhaps the only failing of the reaper is that they require a pace as slow as that of a normal, Texas rig worm. While this impacts the amount of water a splitshotter can cover, it does offer the best chances for success during extremely tough bites.

Splitshotting Lures continued

• *Weenies* - While the straight-tail, 4-inch weenie-style worms have shown their uncanny dominance in vertical, shaking applications, they should not be considered over the curl-tail worm as a splitshotting standard. Yes, they do offer a different "look" and can be very effective under certain conditions. But, for most moving bait situations, a curl-tail lure offers distinct advantages in covering water and providing a natural appearing target for bass.

Like the reaper, the weenie delivers a "change up" to your splitshotting arsenal that should be viewed as a situational lure, not everyday fare.

The Uni-Knot

As with all splitshotting or finesse gear, experience has been the most worthwhile teacher in determining what works best and what just works. After trying a variety of knots, I've settled on the basic Uni-Knot for several reasons:

- *It is a simple knot to tie.*
- *It is an easy knot to tie with light line and cold, wet fingers.*
- *It works.*

In addition to bass, I've caught everything from tuna to marlin using the Uni-Knot without incident. Since the Uni-Knot tightens in the direction of pull, it seems to be a more unified part of the line and lure, rather than merely an abrupt connection between the two.

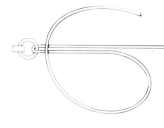

1. Run line through eye of hook at least six inches and fold to make two parallel lines. Bring end of line back in a circle toward hook.

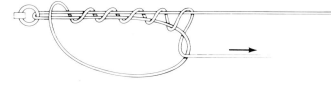

2. Make six turns with tag end around the double line and through the circle. Hold double line at point where it passes through eye and pull tag end to snug up turns.

3. Moisten and pull standing line to slide knot up against eye.

4. Continue pulling until knot is tight. Trim tag end.

The Uni-Knot continued

Other than the basic instructions on how to tie a Uni-Knot, there are two key things to remember:

   • *Always moisten the line when snugging up your knot to avoid crimping your main line.*

   • *As a final step, hold the tag end in your teeth and give a three-way pull (main line, hook and tag end) to cinch everything together. And, don't bite the tag end off! In addition to being bad for your teeth, you'll want to cut the tag off crisply with nippers to provide a short, clean tag to pull the worm over. Without baitholding barbs on the Aberdeen hook, this is an effective way to help keep the worm up on the hook.*

By the very nature of finesse fishing, you can expect to spend more time retying during the day than is necessary in other disciplines. Of course, you'll probably be catching more fish. As a result, you need a knot than can be tied quickly and, most important, one in which you have complete confidence. For me, that's the Uni-Knot.

Tournament Tactics

As a tournament tactic, splitshotting has gained a number of proponents at the club and team tournament levels, but has yet to crack the professional, draw-level circuits. Why? In the first place, very few professional anglers have taken the time to learn the technique and many ascribe to the very same set of myths listed at the beginning of this chapter.

Not long ago, few tournament anglers gave credence to finesse fishing in any form, but things are changing. Drawing from the teachings of Don Iovino, the western "doodling king", Gary Klein has shown what vertical shaking methods can do under the proper circumstances. Splitshotting will also have its day in the sun.

> *What splitshotting does is produce more fish from which to cull a respectable limit.*

But, even if splitshotting never produces a tournament win, it is still one of the most effective measures for producing bass - a lot of bass - when most bass fishermen are putting their boats on their trailers. And, those fish are not always small.

What splitshotting does is produce more fish from which to cull a respectable limit. Yes, you sometimes have to wade through sub-keepers to get those which will measure. But, you will be catching bass that most often are not catchable by any other means. And, if you can turn up an extra keeper or two during slow periods or off days, the advantages seem rather obvious. Particularly in light of the fact that most tournament strategies focus on catching a limit first before switching to big-fish tactics.

Whether you're fishing in a tournament situation or not, a limit in the livewell - of any size - gives you an invaluable boost in confidence. Without question, this "relaxation factor" generally makes one's efforts for the remainder of a day that much more effective. Let's face it, sometimes just getting "bit" often makes all the difference.

In his own words ... George Kramer on Backseat Splitshot

Two thoughts come to mind when I consider splitshotting for bass. One has something to do with the pace of the technique and the other is just how effective it can be in a tournament situation - especially from the back seat of the boat!

Pace is everything in fishing. Although the bass may be responsive at different levels during the day, most fishermen get into trouble when they alter their pace by changing techniques on and off throughout the day. The pace of splitshotting (as a "coverage" method) is one of the easiest to adapt because it isn't "too slow." You're moving the bait - particularly if you're moving it by slow cranking - so you don't get the gnawing feeling that maybe you should be doing something else (using another technique).

An active splitshotter can fish along behind a hardbait tosser, picking targets or else just picking different angles that he wants his bait to come through - and never feel he is being out-gunned. Not only that, the splitshotting technique works wonders, yet is far less strenuous than other methods because you can sit or kneel all the while.

As a tournament technique, splitshotting may be the great equalizer for the "back seater" or non-boat partner. In fact, the more skilled the angler piloting the boat (especially in the wind), the better able he is to control the boat and the more likely the "guy in the back" is going to shine.

The pro who can keep the boat constant over key depths or maintain precise distances from cover is merely putting the back-seat partner's bait in the strike zone longer. If you're in the back seat, you can bet that precision will mean more bass in your bag. And there's nothing the guy up front can do about it!

One of the true pioneers of finesse fishing, George Kramer is a well-published author in magazines, newspapers and books. "Bass Fishing: An American Tradition", a richly illustrated book, is Kramer's most recent bass fishing chronicle.

Why Go Vertical?

California Shakin'

It is of no small irony that the vertical, shakin' technique was developed in California. Just as temblors shudder the California landscape, the shakin' method has begun sending shockwaves through the rest of the bass fishing world. Suddenly, the disbelievers are leaping on the bandwagon as an overwhelming torrent of proof has made the vertical finesse tactics difficult - and foolish - to ignore.

Like splitshotting, shakin' solves a number of bass fishing problems that previously had gone unanswered. Although it is often considered a strictly vertical, deep-water technique, shakin' can be equally effective in shallow water - even for suspended fish away from structure.

The vertical approach requires pinpoint precision.

Designed to take advantage of subtle baits and unaggressive bass, shakin' has evolved into a versatile method that truly captures the very essence of finesse fishing. Here is a method that quite literally force feeds bass that are unwilling to strike anything else, a method that can master the toughest months and the toughest bites for anyone willing to learn.

However, the learning curve in shakin' is considerably longer than the one for splitshotting. While splitshotting can be considered a fish-locating tactic where large areas can be covered quickly, an angler using the more vertical approach must be able to pinpoint the precise location of bass and effectively present a bait to those particular fish.

As a result, there is a greater demand on the fisherman to accurately assess fish behavior, evaluate environmental conditions and effectively use fishing electronics - in addition to delivering a small bait on target to a very specific location. In other words, there is much less margin for error.

This "margin for error" decreases even further as the depth increases and when fish become more lethargic. For the skilled angler, shakin' a bait at 40 feet on a precise piece of structure becomes almost second-nature. Even extreme depths such as 60 or 70 feet are considered workable under the right conditions.

And, just as the shallow water basser becomes very adept at accurately casting 30 or 40 feet on a horizontal plane, the shakin' basser gains an equal degree of proficiency putting baits on target in the vertical format.

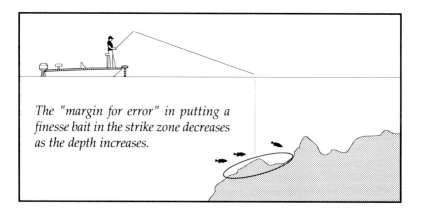

The "margin for error" in putting a finesse bait in the strike zone decreases as the depth increases.

Until finesse fishing tactics came along, most of the vertical fishing applications were reserved for spoon fishermen or anglers using live bait. Generally, bass that were much deeper than 25 or 30 feet and positioned on subtle, outside structure were ignored. Not only were these fish tough to find, but tough to mark and downright brutal to catch.

However, in the deep, clear reservoirs of the West, bass fishermen were faced with a difficult situation. Without much shallow cover in many lakes to hold fish - and seasonal weather patterns that kept most of the fish deep most of the time - learning to catch fish on the vertical format was more a matter of fishing survival than pure creativity.

California Shakin' continued

If it wasn't a fall turnover that pushed the bass deep, it was fishing pressure at the Los Angeles area lakes or the brilliant sunshine and 100-plus temperatures of the Colorado River lakes. Whatever the case, western bass fishermen began turning their attentions to deeper water in the mid 1980s and quickly realized that the early teachings of Buck Perry, "the father of structure fishing," still rang true: *The home of the bass is deep water.*

> *Darter jigging and doodling are different enough to make them very complementary.*

One of the first professionals to popularize deep-water fishing and actually show that consistent catches could be pulled from 40 feet was Don Iovino, the man who developed the "doodling" method. At the same time, other western fishermen were experimenting with various tactics to solve the very same problem. And, from this communal effort arose a jighead/lure combination that seemed to work exceptionally well across a broad range of fishing conditions - the darter jig.

While there have been countless variations on these two themes, darter jig fishing and doodling are still the two most consistent shakin' tactics to emerge from the western experiment. Both have proven themselves under a variety of cicrcumstances, and, perhaps most importantly, have proven themselves in the hands of many, many fishermen.

Best of all, the darter jig and the doodle rig have just enough differences to make them very complementary. The darter has an open hook, the doodle rig is a traditional, Texas style. The darter is fished on spinning tackle, the doodle rig is better with baitcasting gear. The darter jig is a leadhead and the doodle rig uses a slip sinker.

As a result, both darter jigs and doodle rigs should be a part of your finesse repertoire. Anyone who tells you differently is either trying to sell you something or doesn't understand the concept of "versatility."

Why go deep?

Depending on where you fish for bass, you're definition of deep water is a relative one. In Florida, deep water may be a 15-foot ditch cut across a flooded flat. In Nevada, deep-water may be a submerged hump at 60 feet in Lake Mead. Vertical finesse fishing capitalizes on those instances when you can position yourself over the fish, pinpoint their location and fish effectively without spooking them.

For finesse fishermen, vertical methods are the perfect complement to more horizontal, shallow-water tactics like splitshotting. As a general rule-of-thumb, fifteen to twenty feet is, more-or-less, the dividing line between where splitshotting loses its effectiveness and vertical tactics gain theirs. At this depth, it just takes too long for the splitshot rig to descend, the sensitivity of the rig is dulled and the accuracy of the presentation is reduced.

While there are a number of reasons why bass take up residence in deeper water (we'll discuss those later), the reasons why you should fish for them are rather straightforward:

- You must fish where the fish are.

- Deep-water fish receive far less fishing pressure.

- In many parts of the country where the lakes offer deep-water sanctuaries, big bass prefer deep water.

- Vertical techniques are very efficient. With your fishing electronics, you will often see the fish before you catch them. Not just any fish, but the exact fish that ultimately ends up in your livewell.

- In tournament situations, you can dominate a deep-water spot. And, deep-water, finesse patterns are very difficult for other fishermen to duplicate.

Why fish go deep

In the first place, this section should be called "Why fish go shallow" because the natural inclination of bass is to rely on their deep-water sanctuary. Fortunately, the bass don't stay there all of the time and move shallow for various reasons. Of these, the spawning urge is probably the strongest shallow-water influence and one that drives the bass beyond their normal instincts for self-preservation.

Deep-water fish are predictable.

Even in the presence of shallow-water patterns, there are times during the day or over the course of a week when the shallow-water bite turns off. One reason can be that fish use points or other migration routes to move back-and-forth from the shallows to deeper, holding areas making deeper zones the only consistent producers. Another, more common reason is simply that shallow-water fish respond more dramatically to daily weather changes. Whatever the case, deep-water fish are predictable.

What keeps the bass in deep water are several environmental factors such as temperature, light penetration, water clarity and the presence of bait that combine to form a "comfort zone" which the bass find attractive. Again, depending on the type of lake and its geographical location, this deep-water "comfort zone" can vary significantly from region to region and even among lakes within a certain area.

Thermoclines

The one factor that controls most deep-water fishing is the presence of thermoclines - temperature gradients that separate two different temperature layers and control the movement of bass either up or down depending on the time of year. In the summer, thermal stratification sets up in many reservoirs and lakes where shallow water temperatures are too high and deep water temperatures are too low to attract large numbers of bass. Instead, bass will generally seek out the comfort zone just above the thermocline and spend most of their time in the vicinity of this temperature "fence." Occasional forays into the shallows or deep water may occur, but generally are brief, unless the water conditions or forage situation has changed significantly to make a move (shallow or deep) more attractive.

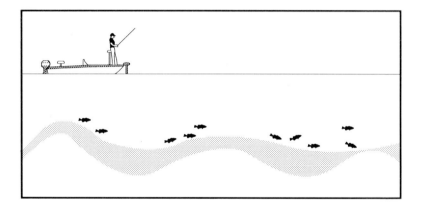

Thermoclines continued

In the fall and winter months following the lake "turnover" - when the upper and lower thermal layers have mixed and re-stratified - the thermocline once again acts as a temperature "fence". This time, the thermocline holds the bass below the "fence" in a comfort zone where the water is warmer than in the upper portion of the lake. However, thermoclines are anything but consistent in strength and thickness of the thermocline layer. It can change dramatically depending on environmental conditions, so avoid making any rigid conclusions about what does and doesn't happen in a particular body of water. You need to be flexible, assess that conditions on a daily basis and go from there.

In both instances, the thermocline layer is an activity zone that attracts both bass and baitfish alike. Obviously, if you are unable to fish effectively in deeper water - in those zones where the fish and baitfish are present - then you will be severely handicapped in your fishing performance. (Actually, the same argument rings true when discussing shallow-water finesse tactics.)

If you are unwilling to learn finesse tactics, you're intentionally limiting your own potential as a fisherman.

In his own words ... Ken Cook on pH and Thermoclines

Water quality, specifically pH and temperature, is the limnological reason that the bass and baitfish are present around deeper, outside structure. The water quality gets right at certain depths because the entire process is powered by the sun. Sunlight penetration is one of the keys to how deep the fish will be.

How deep is deep? The depth of sunlight penetration. This depth controls the growth of phytoplankton (microscopic green plants) that do most of the work to create food for everything else up the food chain. It also has a great bearing on water quality, notably oxygen and pH.

As these microscopic plants grow, they raise the pH. But, when they die, they sink towards the bottom and usually stack up on the thermocline because of the water density differences due to temperature changes.

When water changes temperature, it changes density. And, this density change can cause a layer of dying phytoplankton to stop. This is what you actually read on a depth finder - the phytoplankton stacked on that density change.

As they sit there dying and decaying, it causes a rapid change in the pH level and sometimes the oxygen level. So, you get a pH breakline that is associated with the thermocline. In a lot of cases, this is a real key in determinig where to fish. There is not only proper water quality at that breakline, but it also provides an ambush point and a place for predator bass to feel secure in more stained water. While it may not be a mud line, if you're scuba diving, it is quite visible. It may only be a couple of feet thick, yet it is an obvious band of turbidity. What it amounts to is a major change in water quality especially if you check it out with a temperature gauge or pH meter.

Ken Cook is a former fisheries biologist who became a full-time (and very successful) bass pro with ten Classic® appearances to his credit.

Darter Jigging

Why Darter Jigs?

With the increased interest in light-line, finesse tactics, there has been a deluge of so-called, western shakin' methods. Suddenly, everyone seems to have a drop-dead answer to subtle situations. Unfortunately, a good portion of these western "secrets" are about as authentic as a $5 Navajo rug.

Not that they won't catch fish. They will. But, only under very specific conditions. If you want something that works under a broad range of water, weather and seasonal patterns, there are two basic shakin' methods that outstrip all others when it comes to effectiveness:

> • *When Texas-rigging a bait with glass bead and slip sinker, it's the doodling method popularized by deep-water guru, Don Iovino.*

> • *When using a jig, it's the darter head.*

While the glass bead, doodle rig does offer more in terms of noise production, the exposed hook of the darter rig gives it an obvious advantage in hooksetting. And, clearly, the art of the dart is the easier of the two to learn and to master.

Why Darter Jigs? continued

To many, the darter head appears to be a hybrid leadhead that incorporates some of the straight-fall characteristics of a ball head and the more hydrodynamic, planing action of a banana or slider head. Right on all counts. Except that the term "hybrid" gives the impression that the darter may be the classic jack of all trades and master of none. Fortunately, it is just that, an impression, since the darter jig is exceptionally well-suited for the three basic, shakin'-style applications facing a finesse fisherman.

Rigging the Darter Jig

Of the three most widely-used and proven darter jig techniques, the vertical or near-vertical approach is definitely the most common version as western bassers have turned to the darter jig for years to make something good happen over deep structure, ledges or along steep walls. This is the classic, shakin' tactic.

1. Insert hook point straight down through top of bait.

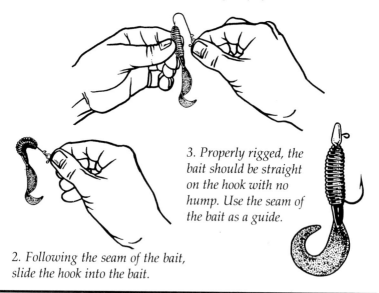

3. Properly rigged, the bait should be straight on the hook with no hump. Use the seam of the bait as a guide.

2. Following the seam of the bait, slide the hook into the bait.

The Classic Shake

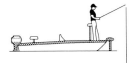

Of the three most widely-used and proven darter jig techniques, the vertical or near-vertical approach is definitely the most common version as western bassers have turned to the darter jig for years to make something good happen over deep structure, ledges or along steep walls. This is the classic, shakin' tactic.

The Shake & Swim

Somewhat less popular, but certainly no less effective is a more horizontal approach which combines the basic, shaking motion of the darter head with a swimming action to alternately shake, swim and shake the darter-rigged grub or worm across a variety of abrupt or subtle changes in bottom contour.

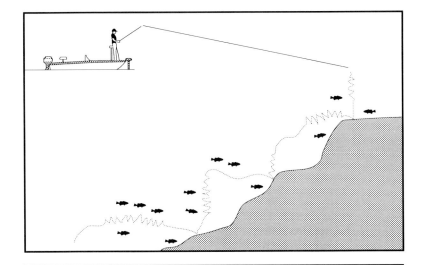

The Swim

In a distant third place is the swimming tactic used by darter jig fisherman to catch suspended or schooling fish away from structure. In this case, the hydrodynamic, bullet-shape of the darter jig can be used to great advantage when moving the bait through non bottom-oriented bass. A productive tactic to be sure, but one that gets much less attention because many bass fishermen have labeled these bass "uncatchable".

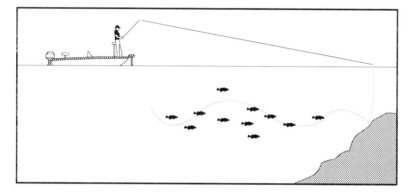

An effective, yet under-used tactic is swimming a darter jig through suspended bass. The jig can be shaken intermittently to encourage strikes.

The Right Start

Although light-line tactics have impressive track records, even the best finesse baits will not produce if not delivered on target. Why? Because darter jigging (and doodling) is roughly comparable to an airplane pilot flying only with instruments. Yes, you can get help from visible, shoreline structure. And, yes, you can consult a topographic map. But, when all is said and done, you still have to depend on your fishing electronics to locate key structure, position your boat effectively and make accurate, vertical presentations. (See Electronics page 111)

Anytime you can find fish deep enough to put your boat over without spooking them, you're in a position to attack with darter jigs. The key is locating bass that are holding on the edge of a break or other bottom irregularity - in other words, fish that appear to be poised in a more positive feeding mode. If there is some bait nearby, so much the better.

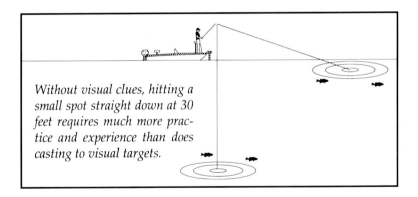

Without visual clues, hitting a small spot straight down at 30 feet requires much more practice and experience than does casting to visual targets.

A marker buoy can be very helpful in marking spots in open water and in helping you to visualize the shape of the contours you're fishing. However, too much of a good thing can work against you as some bassers spend too much time marking and graphing every inch of a selected area. Not only does this slow down the process, but countless boat turns over any area is bound to alert the fish to your presence.

Reaction Baits

Since shakin' with darter jigs is but one way to turn up fish, it is often a wise move to make that first drop on an area with a spoon or lipless crankbait. You'll be surprised how often you can pull one or two aggressive fish off a structure with a reaction-type lure before having to shake them up with worms or grubs.

Pressure Bites

To understand just what you're up against when darter jigging, you must realize that an overwhelming percentage of strikes will be textbook pressure bites. Whether you're bottom bouncing the darter jig or shaking it off structure to suspended fish, rarely do bass attack the darter jig with much fury.

Swings are free:
The best advice in learning to recognize pressure bites is
"If it feels different, swing."

To accurately recreate this delicate sensation, place a rubber band over the thumb and index finger of one hand. Then, close your eyes while stretching and relaxing the rubber band between your two fingers. This is about as close as any demonstration gets to the genuine article. (See Splitshotting, page 18)

In the learning stages, the best advice is simply to swing on anything that feels different. While this may result in several snagged rigs and a few mildly embarassing moments, you'll catch more fish and soon began to differentiate between the pull of a brushpile and that of a bass.

Obviously, a darter strike is gentle enough without anything else deadening the sensation - especially your fishing line. For that reason, a low-stretch monofilament is highly recommended in all darter jig applications. The more direct the connection, the more sensitive the response, the better you'll do with darter jigs.

How to Shake & Set

The shaking motion required (which should be varied like any lure presentation to determine the most productive rhythm) can be compared to tapping your finger on the edge of a table. It is a constant rapping of the darter head against the bottom that is best accomplished with more wrist than rod action.

Instead of moving the rod any great distance, simply get the rodtip briskly moving up and down with sharp shakes of the wrist. While this action should be based more on pure "feel" than anything overly mechanical, the rodtip should only be moving enough to impart a small "U" in the line.

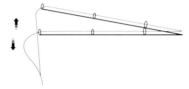

If you are shaking the darter jig properly and putting this "U" in the line, the darter head will be bouncing off the bottom and delivering a very definable dit, dit, dit. The sharp resistance of the small bait will transmit up the line and through the handle of your rod: dit, dit, dit. Then, the strike: dit, dit, dit, duh, duh. Suddenly, the subtle, but recognizable snap of the darter head is replaced with a mushy resistance - a feeling very similar to our rubber band test.

At this point, the open hook advantage of the darter jig comes into play as the thin-wire hooks (normally a 2/0 on the standard 1/8-ounce jig) deliver solid penetration with a minimum of force. Even at depths of 30 or 40 feet, the exposed, thin-wire hooks only require a sharp, forceful pull for adequate hooksets, not an exaggerated swing.

In fact, a powerful hookset in clear water can often create a very negative situation by forcing the fish too quickly to the surface. It has been well-documented that bass hooked in deep, clear water often rocket to the surface uncontrollably when strong pressure is applied. To avoid such problems, an angler need only deliver a firm hookset and then allow the fish to slowly play itself out as it is gently guided to the surface.

Working the Lure

Once you drop the darter rig down to the structure and begin shaking, the need for casting becomes quite minimal. Instead, the trolling motor is used to slowly move the boat - and bait - across the selected area. To account for changes in depth, either to shallow or deep water, you'll need to reel in line or flip open the bail and give out line to maintain direct contact with the bait and the bottom.

When moving your boat over depth changes,
either reel in line or flip open the bail and give out
line to maintain constant bottom contact.

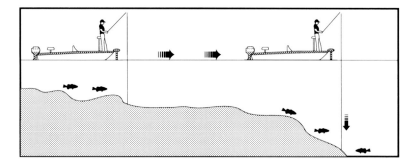

As you become more proficient with the shakin' technique and better able to visualize the structure being fished, the time required to evaluate a particular area or feeding tempo will be reduced. But, shakin' can be just as confusing as any other type of bass tactic. Some days the fish want the bait coming uphill, others downhill. Whatever the case, you need to try several things and correctly determine just how the bass want the lure presented.

An almost guaranteed payoff comes when you feel a small clump of brush on these relatively barren offshore structures. With an exposed hook, your first reaction may be to get out of this impending snag before losing your bait. Resist that temptation at all costs! Just keep shaking and the percentages are in your favor that something good will happen. In fact, a hooked fish may be the only way to get your lure out of the tangle.

Suspended Bass

When the fish are suspended close to structure or when work-ing down a point or bluff, the shake-and-swim method makes the best use of these frequent depth changes.

If fish are suspended, the object is to find a piece of structure close to the fish and at the same depth. The darter rig is cast to this reference structure, allowed to hit bottom and then pulled through the suspended bass.

• If the fish are close to the structure, the lure can be shaken as it is pulled through the strike zone. This is usually quite effective and rather easy to do.

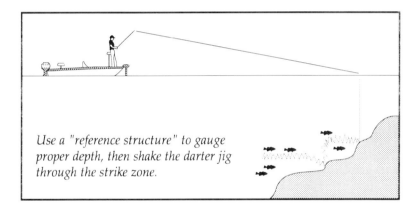

Use a "reference structure" to gauge proper depth, then shake the darter jig through the strike zone.

Suspended Bass *continued*

• If the fish are suspended farther away from structure, the situation becomes more difficult. Instead of shaking the lure off the reference structure, it is better to swim the lure horizontally out to the fish and then begin shaking to keep the bait in the strike zone for as long as possible.

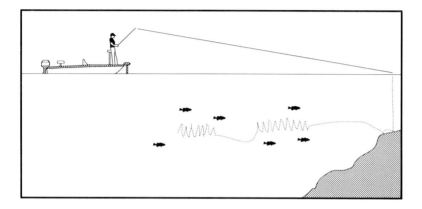

By moving the rod or reeling, swim the darter jig to the fish and then begin shaking to keep the lure in the strike zone.

This is basically the same technique you would use when casting a darter to schooling fish that will not take a surface plug, but are actively feeding on open-water schools of baitfish. While this tactic is much less precise and requires more guesswork from the fisherman, it can be very effective when faced with the prospect of either fishing for suspended bass or blindly pounding the bank.

When the fish are holding at various depths on points or bluffs, the shake-and-swim method involves far more shaking than swimming. And, generally you'll get more fish on the drop than in most other shakin' situations.

Darter Tackle

When it comes to tackle, darter fishing is the quinessential western, light-line, finesse tactic. This is it. Six-pound test, 5 1/2-foot spinning rod, 1/8-ounce finesse fishing at its subtle best.

• *Rods* - In describing the ideal darter rod, you run into the same problems with any light-line gear: What is sensitive? What is too sensitive? Basically, if you have a Gitzit or tube jig rod that works well, the very same rod will do quite nicely for darter jigging - a 5 1/2-foot, medium action spinning rod.

Since all medium actions are not created equal and since most of us do not have the luxury of trying before buying, it is better to lean slightly towards the medium/heavy side of the equation. The operative word in that sentence is "slightly." With six-pound test, you can't afford to overtax the line with rod stiffness. But, a rod that is too limber or has too much action in the tip will only further deaden what is generally a "mush" or "pressure" bite.

Remember, the critical element is rod action, not rod length. Rods longer than 5'6" can work exceptionally well as long as they incorporate a sensitive tip that tapers quickly to a firm midsection and a beefy butt.

• *Reels* - Like splitshotting, darter jigging demands simplicity, smooth performance and balance from a reel. (See Splitshotting, page 28) In fact, the ideal finesse spinning reel is a throwback to reels produced 10 to 20 years ago. No drag systems levers, no fancy spools, no hi-tech styling. Just those things in design and construction which make a smooth-working, durable spinning reel. So, when you find that perfect splitshotting reel, you've also found the right one for darter jigging.

However, you can make a minor concession to innovation in darter jigging by using a reel equipped with an automatic bail trigger. For those who find these triggers acceptable, shaking the darter jig can truly become a one-handed operation with the line depth being adjusted with the touch of a trigger. If you can't get used to the triggers, don't worry. For years, the two-handed method has been serving spinning reel anglers quite nicely.

Shakin' Baits

Of the baits used in darter jig fishing, three plastic versions rise above all others for pure productivity and versatility: the grub, the 4-inch, curly tail worm and the straight-tail weenie.

• Grubs - While it is probably unfair to rate the grub as the big bass bait of the trio, there is something to be said for its bulkier profile and broad-tail action. There is little doubt that the grub offers a larger target for bass and creates more disturbance when moving through the water.

For darter fishing, the grub also offers several advantages in terms of fall rate. By scaling down to a 1/16-ounce jig, the descent of the grub can be slowed dramatically. This is particularly effective when attempting to swim the grub through suspended or schooling fish.

The drawback, however, comes in strike recognition. Without the weight of the jig to help telegraph strikes, a fisherman has to crank up his sensitivity level and become a dedicated line watcher when fishing large bait/small jig combinations.

Shakin' Baits continued

• Four-inch, curly tail worms - For delicacy and slow-speed action, the four-inch curly tail worm has long been a solid producer for darter jig fishermen. However, not all worms have the prerequisite tail action that works well - or at all - during the subtle shaking action of a darter jig.

If you have any questions at all about the performance of a plastic worm, buy the smallest amount possible and give them a bathtub test at home. Better yet, get the store manager to rig one on a darter jig and test it out in the shop aquarium.

For darter jig applications, the curly tail worm is best suited for suspended fish or working more horizontally across structure where the fluttering action of the tail truly makes a difference.

Shakin' Baits continued

• Weenies - In more vertical pursuits, there is probably no better darter jig bait than the straight-tail, four-inch weenie. What began as a Southern California phenomenon has spread across the country faster than a Kansas prairie fire and brought legions of bass fishermen into the world of finesse fishing.

While weenie-style worms have been around for years, they did not take off in popularity until handpour specialists began producing "green weenies" in what appeared to be a rather uninspiring, greenish brown color. However, the few Southern Cal bassers who didn't believe in the weenie were soon pummeled into submission by the incredible catches accredited to this straight-tail bait.

Soon, the green weenie became blue, red, purple, chartreuse and plenty of other hues as California bassers experimented with their new-found weapon. Eventually, the demand for weenies so far outstripped the supply available through handpour worm makers that one manufacturer, the Kalin Company, set its sights on "weeniedom" with mechanically laminated worms that added firetails to the equation.

So far, the hits just keep on coming with the weenie. The reason? As a darter jig, shakin' bait the weenie delivers a very subtle, natural undulation that somehow triggers a strike response in bass. In a fishing discipline where the bass are more-or-less being force fed something they really don't want to eat, the weenie certainly validates the adage that less is more. If you try to get more technical than that, you're just guessing.

Shakin' Baits continued

• Midget jig 'n pig - The one non-plastic darter rig that has proven to be a worthy addition is nothing more than a scaled-down jig 'n pig. Although it can be effective on largemouths, it is particularly deadly for smallies.

For this miniature version of the jig 'n pig, the only extra materials you'll need (other than some darter heads) are tying thread and some super-thin, rubber skirt material. It is very important to use the thinnest possible rubber since the hackle portion of the skirt (the section that points forward) must pulse back and forth when the lure is moved through the water.

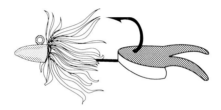

Sweetened with No. 101 Uncle Josh pork, this pint-size jig 'n pig can be fished on six-pound test much like its larger cousin. But be forewarned - like all shakin' baits, the hits come as pressure bites, not the standard tap, tap of a jig strike.

As you gain more confidence in the shakin' technique you'll wonder how you ever got by without a darter jig. Like its slip sinker counterpart for Texas rigs, the darter jig has become part and parcel to this thing we call finesse.

In his own words ... Gary Klein on Darter Jigging

To me finesse fishing is small baits, light weight and light line. Usually the reason we use these techniques is because the conditions dictate finesse-type baits - conditions like clear water and frontal conditions.

Normally the light line will result in more strikes, but not necessarily bigger fish. However, I have surprised myself with the size of fish I've taken on 6-pound test line, some over 8 pounds.

Finesse fishing means 6- or 8-pound test line. I've never dropped to 4-pound test because I don't feel there is much difference between four and six. This forces you to use an ultralight outfit which usually means a six-foot, medium action graphite rod with a well-balanced spinning reel.

The best weights for darter heads are 1/8 or 1/16-ounce with the grub, Gitzit and small, curl-tail worm - the three top lure choices.

One of the advantages to darter heads is being able to crazy glue the worm to the jig and use the weight-forward design of the darter for skipping versus a Texas rig with a slip sinker. If you're fishing around boat docks, the ability to skip a Gitzit or 4-inch worm is very important at times. So, it is an advantage to have that weight forward design.

The other advantage to using a darter head is the action. With the weight that far forward of the bait, it makes the lure dip real quick. If you skip a Gitzit (with an exposed jighead), the bait will roll over and begin its spiral fall more quickly than if the head was inserted in the Gitzit. So, remember, by using a jighead on the outside - like a darter head - versus putting it on the inside, you are changing the action a little.

Another advantage to the darter head comes around shale, rock or pea gravel and when lower water temperatures or a sluggish bite demands a slower presentation. It's almost like dragging a splitshot rig, but I'm actually dragging a darter head. The reason I like that jig exposed is simply for the clicking sound it

Gary Klein continued

makes on the bottom. It's just a little added noise that attracts the fish.

Still another advantage to the long tapered nose of a darter head is the added planing surface it gives to those little 4-inch, straight-tailed worms I shake a lot. It adds a darting action in addition to coming through the fish's mouth (because of the taper) for better hooksets.

What my tournament success with darter heads accomplished was to enlighten bass fishermen about finesse fishing. I showed them the advantages of fishing finesse baits at the proper time. So far in my career, I've won three major events fishing finesse equipment - the U.S. Open, 1985 B.A.S.S. tournament at Lake Lanier and in 1988 at the B.A.S.S. Bull Shoals Arkansas Invitational.

At each time, it was a condition that dictated finesse tactics. Being raised on the west coast, I have a strong background in clear, deep water, finicky fish and not a lot of strikes.

Without a doubt, it's an advantage. With finesse equipment, I don't have to test it or get used to it. I can pick up a doodle rod and win tomorrow with it. Or, I can win five years from now. In my 18-year career, I've literally caught thousands and thousands of fish on ultralight outfits and finesse baits. So, this is an advantage.

I think it's harder for an angler to downsize his equipment, not only physically, but mentally. It's easier for an angler used to finesse stuff to pick up a "bubba" outfit - the long rods and heavy line - and be a little more aggressive. That's more forgiving in the long run than the finesse techniques.

Perhaps the most versatile tournament professional, Gary Klein is as comfortable with a flippin' stick as he is with a finesse rod. Using his exceptional talents and experience in western finesse tactics, Gary was the first to show the value of darter jigs in tournament competition.

Doodling

Why Doodling?

In the hands of its inventor, California pro basser Don Iovino, "doodling" has become an art form. Right down to the carefully painted brass slip sinkers, colored glass beads and laminated "doodle worms", Iovino has created a mini industry from his own invention.

To his credit, Iovino has not only managed to forge a credible tournament career from his brainstorm, but impressive tackle sales that point up one very clear fact: To be a complete bass fisherman, you have to know how to catch fish deep.

While darter jig fishing is much easier to learn and less complicated from a tackle standpoint, doodling is an important, deep-water option worthy of your time. And, the differences between these two methods actually make them very compatible techniques.

The Noise Factor

Perhaps the key advantage in the Texas-rigged, doodle setup is the addition of a glass bead between the slip sinker and hook. Although the color and flash add to the presentation, it is the noise factor that makes the fire-polished glass beads important.

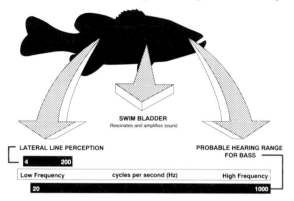

SWIM BLADDER
Resonates and amplifies sound

LATERAL LINE PERCEPTION

4   200

PROBABLE HEARING RANGE
FOR BASS

Low Frequency   cycles per second (Hz)   High Frequency

20   1000

With a shaking motion comparable to that of a darter head, the doodle worm is shaken continuously in a subtle, but forceful manner. With each shake of the rodtip, the glass bead and slip sinker clack together to create a sound that has proven quite attractive to bass. Whether it duplicates the click of a crawdad or simply triggers the curiosity of a fish in a general way is still up for debate.

What is known about sound and bass is this: With an inner ear mechanism to hear high-frequency sound, a lateral line to process low-frequency vibrations and a swim bladder to reso-nate these sounds, the bass is especially well-equipped to process sound in its environment. And, since sound travels five times faster through water, bass function in a world where sound is often the first indication of forage or danger.

Adding to the noise factor of the doodle rig, Iovino has im-proved upon the sinker/bead combination by substituting brass slip sinkers for lead ones. For centuries, the sound quali-ties of brass have been well-documented and now find a unique place in the angling arts. While this is but a subtle alteration, Iovino's doodle rig involves a host of minor variations from the norm which, in total, can add up to deep-water success.

The Presentation Factor

While the basic presentation and techniques required are very similar to those discussed in Section 3, Darter Jigging, the bait offered to the fish reacts differently because of the standard Texas/slip sinker rig. Instead of the weight-forward darter jig which pulls the weenie down in a vertical or planing descent, the slip sinker arrangement brings the bait back to earth in more of a looping, disjointed manner. While these differences are subtle, they can make a huge difference depending on the feeding nature of the bass.

Also, the doodle rig is obviously more weedless which allows for better presentations over brushy terrain or chunk rock. In such instances, if you're getting snagged repeatedly, the darter head can become a real liability.

Doodling Gear

Perhaps the greatest difference between darter jigging and doodling is in the rod and reel used. For doodling, a medium action, fast taper baitcasting rod is preferred - one that offers a sensitive tip, a firm mid-section and a beefy butt. Without the exposed hook of a darter head, the doodle rig demands a more forceful hookset to drive the hook through the plastic bait. Although some fishermen have found spinning gear acceptable, the most proven formula for doodling is baitcasting gear.

The baitcasting reel used is equally important. In fact, Iovino has created a cottage industry of sorts in reworking Garcia "round reels" like the 3400C to make them perform beyond the specifications of straight, factory models. The onus here is clearly on a very free-working freespool that allows the bait to descend quickly to the 40 and 50-foot ranges often plied by doodlers. Whatever brand you choose, however, make sure the freespool is tuned out for maximum spin. Remember, in deep-water fishing, your casts are actually vertical "drops" where backlash control is not a factor. Also, be sure to use a reel with a flawless drag system. With light line, there is very little margin for error.

Terminal Tackle

• Hooks - For weenie-style doodle worms, a 1/0 sproat hook is considered standard fare. Of course, should a larger bait be used, you'll need to size up accordingly.

• Slip sinkers - In most instances, a 3/16-ounce slip sinker will be the best choice. But, in situations where wind or current reduce bottom contact, a 1/4 to possibly a 5/16-ounce sinker can be substituted. The important thing to remember is that by sizing up too far, you may be taking the bait - and your presentation - out of the finesse category thereby reducing its effectiveness.

• Glass beads - First, make sure they are made of glass for proper sound qualities. Second, be sure the glass beads are fire-polished to prevent line abrasion. Third, find the most productive hues for the conditions encountered.

• Line - While brand may be a personal choice, line size should not. Either 6 or 8-pound test clear line should be used. Since the goal in doodling (or any finesse method for that matter) is subtlety, heavier tests can greatly degrade the performance of delicate doodling baits. Plus, the need for stronger line is generally negated by the lack of cover found at greater depths.

• The worm - The doodle worm is a 4-inch, straight-tail weenie-style laminated worm that offers subtle coloration and equally subtle action. Unlike curl-tail worms, the doodle worm is very "technique dependent." In other words, the action of the doodle worm is generated by the angler. There is no design factor that creates action when the bait is moved - only the rodwork of the fisherman.

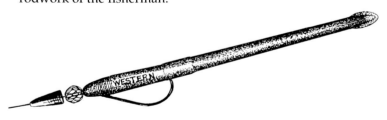

Topo Tactics

In doodling, boat position is everything. After all, instead of making 40-foot casts to a visible target where your accuracy can immediately be determined, vertical drops to a small target area can be far off the mark without any indication except, of course, for lack of results. To enhance your bait targeting efforts, a review of the Electronics section (page 111) is in order - for without a strong, working knowledge of your electronics, your efforts will find only very limited success.

Equally critical to your doodling success is a quality topographic map and your ability to interpret it. No longer will you always have the luxury of visible structure to serve as a guide. Nor will you have visible cover to mark the way back to a spot. Instead, the topo map will become your deep-water bible and underwater road atlas.

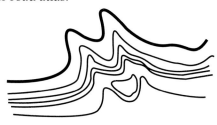

Just as topo maps can depict the Rocky Mountains in lines that show both gradual and abrupt elevation changes, marine topo maps show the very same changes in depth of a lake bottom. Called contour lines, the lines of a topo map are usually separated in five-, 10- or 20-foot increments. The smaller the increment, the more detailed the map.

The contour interval will be printed on the map right along with the high water elevation of the lake at maximum pool. In times of high water or drought where the lake level can be dramatically higher or lower than normal, a phone call to the marina manager or lake office can give you the current level. Determining the current water level gives you an accurate starting point from which to judge the actual depth of structure. By doing so, you'll be able to tell where the land ends and the water begins regardless of the changes above or below normal lake levels.

Topo tactics continued

On the topo map, the more space between the lines, the more gradual the slope. Lines closer together show areas of faster depth change. So, when you see well-spaced lines that extend far from shore, you can quite rightly assume this area to be gently sloping with no pronounced changes in depth. However, a couple of well-spaced lines followed by lines that nearly touch one another very clearly depict a sloping shoreline that drops off quite abruptly. If the contour lines are stacked one atop the other right next to shore, you can expect to find a cliff, steep wall or very sharp dropoff in this area.

Similarly, submerged points or islands out from shore can just as easily be identified as having sloping or abrupt depth changes by how far apart, or how close together, the contour lines appear on the topo map. Just how gradual or how abrupt the changes may take a little on-the-water comparison - comparing the map to the genuine article through the use of your sonar.

In some cases, a topo map can even give you an indication of the bottom composition. For instance, sharp, steep drops obviously will contain more rock than shallow, sloping areas.

Assuming you've done your homework on the prevailing conditions and seasonal patterns, a topo map should clearly show you some obvious starting points. Submerged islands, humps, extended points, and dropoffs are just some of the deep-water structure that can be found on a topo map.

However, while doodling can be an offshore, isolated endeavor, you should not completely detach yourself from the shoreline. The terrain surrounding the lake is simply the dry portion of the stuff you're trying to visualize below the surface. If the shoreline features a jagged, rock-strewn point above the water, you can bet that the underwater portion of this same point looks very, very similar. And, if you follow the angle of a point or the cut of a gully into the water, you can, with some certainty, figure out just how far that point or cut extends out into the lake.

Moving the Bait

As with all fishing aids, the topo map is only as helpful as you want to make it. Discovering the subtleties of a lake, those small areas within an area that hold the most or largest bass, takes time.

Once a suitable area has been located, you often need to mark the location with buoys to have some reference points in open water. As discussed earlier, overdoing the buoy thing can waste time and stir up an area unnecessarily. So, keep things simple, visualize the structure to be fished and work methodically.

Taking into consideration any wind or current, make your drop and then use your trolling motor to slowly move the lure across the fish-holding structure. In any good doodling area, the ledges and dropoffs present will force you to constantly take in or let out small amounts of line to maintain bottom contact. The shaking motion (Darter Jigging, page 57) is continued throughout these movements of boat and line.

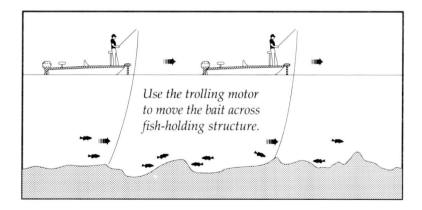

Use the trolling motor to move the bait across fish-holding structure.

During this fishing "ballet", you'll want to keep a very watchful eye on your electronics since many of the fish caught while doodling (unlike most other bass fishing methods) are the ones you'll see on the flasher or sonar screen.

While it sounds like a lot to do all at once, with practice this delicate movement of the lure can be very fluid and very fruitful.

The Doodling Hookset

Like darter jigging, most doodling strikes will be dull, pressure bites as the bass gently inhales the worm and holds it. When the strike is felt, the hookset is made with a forceful, but fluid upwards sweep of the rod.

Since the rod should be pointed horizontal or towards the water, there isn't any need to take up line and reel down. When the hook is driven home, you'll need to reel quickly since the natural tendency of deep-water fish is to come up, especially in clear water.

In crystal clear water situations such as those found at Mead or Powell, deep-water bass not only head toward the surface following the hookset, they rocket upwards like a finned Polaris missile. When this happens, a fisherman finds himself unable to reel fast enough to keep slack out of the line.

To prevent lost fish in clear water, you should relax pressure after the hookset and allow the fish to fight himself out as you deliberately bring him up. But, in all situations, you should be ready to reel quickly following the hookset to keep ahead of a fish zooming to the surface.

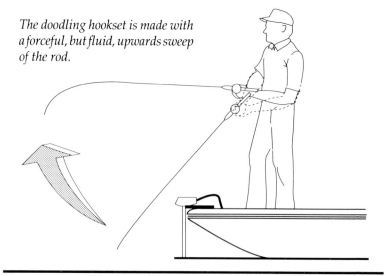

The doodling hookset is made with a forceful, but fluid, upwards sweep of the rod.

Doodling and the Spoon

When you find deep-water fish poised on the edge of a break or near baitfish, a spoon such as the Hopkins, Luhr-Jensen Crippled Herring or Haddock models can be used to pick off aggressive feeders. Often, Iovino will make his first drop with a spoon to take advantage of these fish.

Care of Deep-Caught Bass

The problem in catching deep-water bass is one of decompression, where the fish is taken so quickly from its acclimated depth that it is unable to adjust to changes in water pressure.

When this happens, the swim bladder (a gas-filled sac located just above the stomach and used to regulate buoyancy) becomes distended and can be forced out of the fish's mouth. Less noticeable, but equally serious, is damage to blood vessels causing trauma to tissue and bleeding. Outward symptoms of this are bloody fins and protruding eyes.

In many cases, instant release of the fish is all that is necessary to insure survival. But, if a bass cannot maintain a normal swimming position, needle deflation should be performed at once. Even fish taken as shallow as 15 feet might require needle deflation, says Dennis Lee, a fisheries biologist for the California Department of Fish and Game and someone who has conducted studies on deep-caught bass. Care should be taken to observe the condition of bass taken even at these more shallow depths since the fish may have momentarily come up from greater depths to feed.

While some believe that slow playing deep-water bass is an effective way to lessen decompression damage, there is evidence that this technique may be even more stressful to bass. Of the methods used on deep-water bass, the most effective is needle deflation where a hypodermic needle is inserted through the skin and into the body cavity. Done properly, the needle will puncture the gas bladder allowing the gas to escape.

Care of Deep-Caught Bass continued

According to Lee, the best method of locating the point of insertion is to "draw an imaginary line from the notch separating the spiny ray and soft ray portions of the dorsal fin downward to the anal opening. Insert the needle (minimum two inches in length) along this line approximately midway between the lateral line and the anal opening."

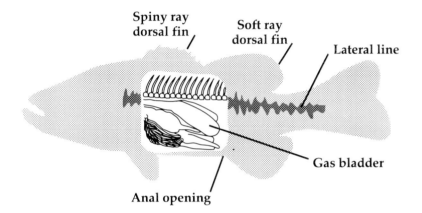

In his own words ... Don Iovino on Doodle Sliding

People always think you have to doodle deep, but you don't. The doodle slide is a method which allows you to fish very shallow by shaking the worm down, pulling off breaklines and catching a high percentage of suspended bass.

With doodle sliding, change your sinkers to 1/8-ounce from 0 to 10 feet, 5/32 from 10 to 20 feet and from 20 on go to the 3/16-ounce using 6 or 8-pound test.

The object is to keep the bait off the bottom in a natural mode. Once it sets down, let it rest for just a second, barely pull as if you were splitshotting and then start shaking it again. Often, after you let the bait sit for a moment and start shaking again, the bass nail it.

Doodle sliding allows you to work a variety of cover and structure situations, particularly when the bass are suspended just off breaks. But, these breaklines don't have to be dramatic, nor do they have to be deep.

Remember, deep is a relative thing. You just have to adapt the doodling technique in its various phases to the type of environment you're fishing. A bass is a bass. Rethink what deep is based on the lake you're fishing. If 15 feet is a deep lake in Oklahoma, then fish the breakline from 10 to 15 feet. That's the "deep." If you go to Missouri and 35 feet at Table Rock is the depth to fish, then doodle there.

On the subject of how spoons fit into my overall technique, I use them to key on shad, especially in August and September when the shad are very active. I simply throw out a spoon and retrieve it as I would a jig. To avoid hanging up, I switch to a single hook on the spoon.

Or, I'll throw it out in open water (with treble hooks) and retrieve it very slowly with the rodtip down. I use slow motions with the reel handle, almost "dead sticking" it right through the baitzone.

Don Iovino is a top western pro and inventor of the doodling method.

Tube Jigs

Tubing

A proven performer that can add a subtle touch to your finesse arsenal is the the tube jig or Gitzit, originally developed and popularized by western pro basser, Bobby Garland. Created largely out of necessity (Garland needed a delicate bait that could entice skittish bass in ultra-clear desert impoundments), it is no coincidence that the tube jig resembles an overgrown crappie jig. As part of an early tackle business, Garland invented a split-tail tube jig for crappie and simply enlarged upon his idea to produce a bass lure that has since gained a formidable fish-catching reputation.

As the tube jig gained national prominence, bass professionals such as Guido Hibdon and Shaw Grigsby found even more ways to make the tube jig work its subtle wonders.

The Tube Jig

Fished in its purest form, the tube jig is best classed as a "jump" bait rigged with a 1/16 or 1/8-ounce leaded tied to either 6 or 8-pound test line. Although there are a number of rigging variations, the standard format is with the leadhead jig inside the plastic tubular body of the lure.

Two Tube Rigs

1. **With a standard jig head,** *moisten and insert into the skirt end of tube. Push jig head into tube until it touches closed end. Pop the eye of the hook through the plastic, taking special care to align the hook shank with the bait. (A poorly aligned jig may cause the tube to spiral excessively.)*

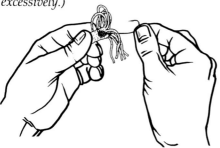

2. Depending on the length of the hook shank, the point of the hook may have to be inserted through the plastic (just above the skirt) to produce a properly rigged tube - one that is straight without any arch or "hump."

1. **With a tapered leadhead,** *the hook point is inserted through the top edge of the tube (where the hook eye will be positioned). The hook is pivoted and pushed into the tube. The hook is then pushed through the side of the tube making sure to align the hook shank with the bait.*

Texas Rigging

As the use of tube jigs spread around the country, fishermen began devising methods to make the tube more effective for their particular brand of bass fishing. More cover or vegetation demanded a more weedless hook arrangement. Mono, wire and fiber guards have all been added to jigheads and do provide a degree of weedlessness. Without question, they can be very effective and should be considered in your tube jig tactics.

But, whatever jig arrangement is used, it is still a jig. It falls like a jig and swims like a jig. Like the differences between darter jigging and doodling, the addition of a slip sinker to a bait does make a difference; not only in how the bait goes through cover, but in how it looks to the fish.

By Texas rigging a tube jig, you add to your versatility and increase the amount of water you can fish effectively. And, with the advent of such hook systems as Shaw Grigsby's HP Hooks, the difficulty in rigging and keeping a tube on the hook has been eliminated.

These unique hooks are equipped with a special clip that holds the tube in place and a Kahle hook that sports a huge gap to ensure solid hooksets. An additional benefit of the HP Hook is in the number of fish which can be caught on a single tube before it is rendered unusable.

Shaw Grigsby's High Performance hook

Texas Rigging continued

Another Texas-style rigging method comes by way of California pro Rich Tauber who utilizes a 3/0 offset Gamakatsu hook to effect a weedless pitchin' and flippin' rig. The offset bend of the shank helps keep the tube up on the hook which is inserted through the top edge of the tube bait. This is the very same way you would begin rigging a plastic worm. The difference comes when the hook is turned to reinsert the point into the bait. Instead of imbedding the point into the tube, the length of this 3/0 hook allows you to simply rest the hook point in the opening of the tube.

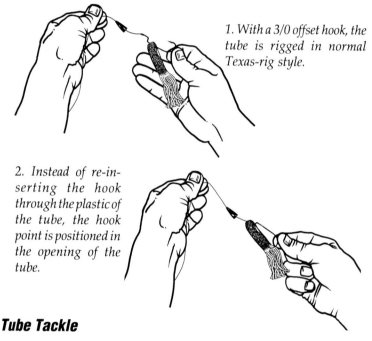

1. With a 3/0 offset hook, the tube is rigged in normal Texas-rig style.

2. Instead of re-inserting the hook through the plastic of the tube, the hook point is positioned in the opening of the tube.

Tube Tackle

When fishing light lines and tube jigs (generally in open water or sparse cover conditions), the rod of choice is a 5 to 6-foot, medium action spinning rod. However, this is not to infer that a tube jig rod is without "backbone." Actually, the proper tube rod is a blend of sensitivity and strength - one that provides enough "tip" to feel the bait and transmit strikes without sacrificing "beef" in the midsection and butt for power and control.

The Delivery

Whether you're fishing a tube off ledges or weedlines, most strikes will come on the fall. As a result, the accomplished tube fisherman becomes a dedicated line watcher.

To simplify this line watching and maintain the rod in a strike-ready position, the action of the tube can be controlled solely by the reel. Whether you're fishing along a steep wall, off the bottom or working open water for suspended fish, cranking the reel imparts the required "jumping" action to the tube while allowing the fisherman to concentrate on the line and lure. Just as if you were moving your rod, the action of the tube can be varied with the cranking of the reel.

While the tube jig can be presented effectively with rod movement, this method of controlling the jig with the reel simply keeps the rod always at a strike-ready position and makes for a higher strike-to-hookup percentage.

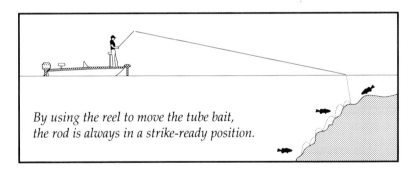

By using the reel to move the tube bait, the rod is always in a strike-ready position.

If you prefer to work the bait with rod movement, Bobby Garland's weigh-the-line technique is very effective.

Weighing the line

Popularized by Bobby Garland, one method of controlling tubes with rodwork is a jump-and-fall method where the angler "weighs" the line each time the rod is lifted to move the bait. If the line feels "heavier", it's time to set the hook. This method of strike detection combined with rod movement is very similar to the identification of "pressure bites" when fishing splitshot or darter rigs.

But, whether you choose to control the tube with rod or reel action, the basic jump-and-fall presentation remains the same. This tantalizing motion usually triggers a strike on the fall, so be ready.

Swimming the tube

One of the more common instances where rodwork comes into play is when an angler makes the tube "swim" over snags or rockpiles and then allows the bait to drop into the attack zone. This swimming action is done with the rod held in a relatively high position. Then, when the tube is over the strike zone, the rod is lowered to allow the lure to fall vertically. But, even in this slack line situation, the bow in the line should always be under control. In fact, in virtually every tube jig method, the concept of "controlled slack" is the key element in proper lure presentation.

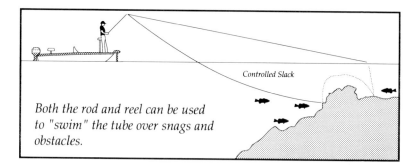

Controlled Slack

Both the rod and reel can be used to "swim" the tube over snags and obstacles.

Controlled slack

Controlled slack is equally crucial in recognizing strikes. When fishing tube baits, the strike can vary dramatically from an abrupt "jump" of the line to the pure "mush" of a pressure bite. In many cases, the only indication is the movement of the line itself as a bass sucks in the tube and slowly moves off.

Done properly, controlled slack allows the tube to fall vertically, unimpeded by any pressure on the line. There are no coils of line on the surface or lazy curves of line between you and the lure. Instead, the connection should be straight and direct. Then, even if a bass takes a tube on the fall, it can only swim a short distance before you notice some line movement.

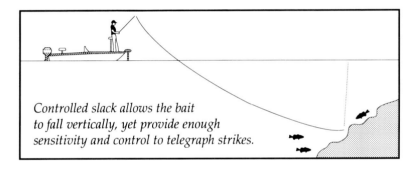

Controlled slack allows the bait to fall vertically, yet provide enough sensitivity and control to telegraph strikes.

With too much slack, a bass can take the tube and move off. By the time you are aware of its presence, the angle between you and the bass can turn hooksetting into a real adventure. While bass will hold onto tube baits much longer than most conventional plastics, it still may not make up for a late strike and a weird angle. Especially if the bass makes a left turn at the first tree trunk.

However, if a bass takes the bait and your slack is out-of-control, don't smoke the gears in your reel trying to crank down for a hookset. Instead, reel up the slack quickly, but deliberately, and feel the weight of the bass before you set the hook. By doing so, you'll have a direct line to the fish and much better odds for a solid hookset.

Shakin' the tube

In deeper-water situations, the tube can be fished in a shaking manner similar to darterheading or doodling. Depending on the depth, wind and current, you'll probably want to increase the weight of the jighead from the normal shallow-water weights of 1/16 and 1/8-ounce to a heavier 1/4-ounce version. This will help you maintain that critical contact between lure and angler, especially when fishing vertical where the hits are little more than a mushy or weightless feeling.

Depth control

But, whether you're shaking or jumping the tube, another key factor in lure presentation is proper depth control. If fish are holding in 10 feet of water, it is time-consuming and inefficient to cast repeatedly into two feet of water to bring the lure to fish holding in 10 feet. Granted, a few fish will be taken at other depths, but the experienced fisherman always plays the percentages.

As a result, veteran anglers will first identify the most productive depth range, position their boat over that depth and work parallel to the shore or structure. The result? A lure that is in the attack zone on each and every cast.

Glide for suspended bass

While catching suspended fish is never a sure thing, the tube lure does offer some possibilities, whether bass are holding off ledges, over treetops or in open water.

When bass are suspended near a dropoff or break, it is generally better to change from the parallel casting format to one where the tube is pitched up shallow and worked downhill. As the lure falls off the ledge into deeper water, extend your arms and point the rod at the water. Then, the rod is slowly pulled up and back to glide the tube lure horizontally through the fish. In such cases, your electronics can show the precise relationship of suspended bass to the structure and help give you the patience to experiment with various retrieves and jig weights.

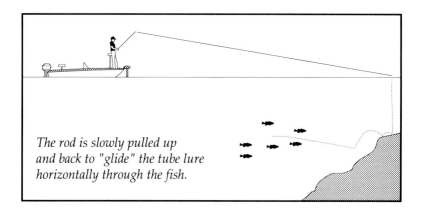

The rod is slowly pulled up and back to "glide" the tube lure horizontally through the fish.

Open Water

In open-water situtations where there is no point-of-reference (like a dropoff) for accurate presentations, finding the proper depth basically involves some trial and error. Although it may be less efficient, the jump-and-fall method previously described is a better method of locating fish. Then, the glide cast can be used more effectively.

Shade

During midday fishing conditions when you're working shore-line areas such as ledges or sheer rock faces, a crucial element in making effective presentations is shade. This is especially important in clear water, minimal cover conditions where the only cover element is shade. Unless the bass dictate otherwise, shaded pockets (even a sliver of shade along a cliff face or next to a submerged boulder) should always be a top priority in bright, sunshine conditions.

River Tubing

In tackling a river environment, the standard jump-and-fall method can be used along with a "dead stick" tactic that uses the current to impart the action. However, this is not to imply that the tube is hauled along, trolling style, behind the boat. Instead, the tube is delivered to the target area with a quartering cast upstream and allowed to drift, bump and bounce as it moves with the current.

To maintain that critical "controlled slack" in river situations, the boat either should be holding its position against the current or slowly moving upstream via the trolling motor. A straight, downstream drift tactic can be used, but the chances of getting snagged with every cast increase dramatically.

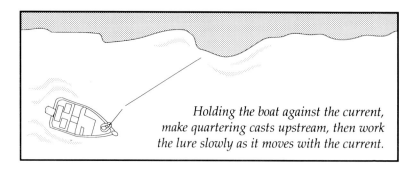

Holding the boat against the current, make quartering casts upstream, then work the lure slowly as it moves with the current.

Backreeling

As in most all finesse methods, the tactical advantage gained by backreeling (see page 22) when tube fishing cannot be over-stated. While drag systems on spinning reels have improved dramatically over the years, there is no mechanical method more sensitive than your own sense of touch. Sure, it requires a little practice - practice which can be gained on bass caught in non-tournament, non-critical situations - but it is time well-spent. Since you've taken the time to learn the subtleties of finesse fishing, you owe it yourself to explore all the possibilities.

Topwater Backup

One of these possibilities - which has been proven many times by veteran anglers - is the effectiveness of tube jigs as a backup bait for topwater fishing. Following missed strikes or even for foraging bass that come up too fast for topwater presentations, the tube is an excellent means of drawing "come back" strikes. The key element here, however, is in getting the tube back on the fish quickly. To do this, you should have a tube rod rigged, ready and set aside for rapid, follow-up casts.

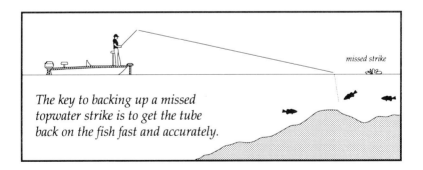

The key to backing up a missed topwater strike is to get the tube back on the fish fast and accurately.

Depending on the situation, you may want to upsize in jig weight if the fish are breaking any distance from the boat. Again, there is some experimentation required since the bass may strike the instant the tube hits the water or it may require some rodwork to draw a response.

In his own words ... Shaw Grigsby on Sight Fishing

To me, sight fishing is the ultimate. It's not just fishing, since there is actually a lot of hunting involved. You have to see the fish before it sees you. You have to present a bait without the fish knowing you're there.

In other types of fishing, it's as if the fish suddenly appears on your line. With sight fishing, you see him ahead of time and then you have to plan your strategy. Skillwise, it's very challenging.

The first misconception is everyone thinks sight fishing is simply catching spawning fish in the springtime. I use tube baits all year long. It represents both a shad and a crawfish, two major food sources for predacious fish.

Of course, during certain times of the year, the fish may position themselves in deep water to where you don't get a lot of fish up shallow. Overall, sight fishing is primarily a spring and fall, clear water, shallow water tactic. But, many fish come up to feed and cruise the shallows, even in the heat of the summer - so try not to limit yourself.

The basic requirements for sight fishing are clear water and a great pair of sunglasses. For tackle, you need light line in the 6 to 10-pound test range, better presentations, longer casts and spinning equipment. Line tests vary with the situation and the cover. For instance, in spring when larger fish are expected, I may size up to 10-pound test. For summer or fall fishing around docks, I may use six pound.

I'll put my trolling motor on high, head down the banks and just start looking. Obviously I would be throwing other types of classic clear-water baits like a jerkbait (Bang-O-Lures, Rattlin' Rogue, Bomber Long A), floating worm or Slug-Go-style bait instead of the tube lure. But, even when I'm catching fish on these baits, I'm always looking for sight fish.

One of my keys to sight fishing is presenting the bait naturally with the most natural presentation being the one that is slow. So, if you throw out a bait with a heavy weight and it falls right to the bottom, to me, that's not very natural. I've noticed that the

Shaw Grigsby on Sight Fishing *continued*

fish I'm after don't go for that presentation very often.

For the most part, I throw 1/16 or 1/32 weights with tube jigs. To me, a 1/8-ounce weight is pretty heavy since the objective is to put the tube on target with a minimum of splash. Another reason for using such light weights is to duplicate the slow fall of an injured minnow or the gentle descent of a crawdad as it settles back to the bottom. Again, the most natural presentation.

Every fish is different. They're all individuals.
You'll work a fish and from his fin movements and attitude,
you can tell he is aggressive.
You say to yourself "I can catch this fish."

When looking at a sight fish, you have to develop a mental image of what you are going to do. If he's cruising down a bank, you've got an advantage, he's moving. You can throw ahead of him so he moves up towards the bait. If the fish is just hanging out in a bush, you have to figure out how to present the bait without spooking him. You may have to go way past him and work the bait back to him. It gets harder because you may have to pull the bait through the bush. Sometimes, it's a very tricky deal.

There are plenty of situations where you only have one chance and your cast better be perfect. Sometimes you have to use a sidearm cast or an underhand pitch. Or, you have to peg a 1/32-ounce sinker and skip it on top of the water like a spooked minnow.

Once you get his attention, then you have to convert it into a strike. Twitch the bait, barely drag it, pop it, nudge it. Anything you can think of.

But, make one wrong move and you'll lose the fish. Maybe you moved it two inches and you shouldn't have moved it at all. Maybe you should have just barely nudged it. Whatever the case, once the fish turns off of it, he's done. You can cast a dozen more times, follow the fish down the bank and keep pestering

Shaw Grigsby on Sight Fishing *continued*

him, it doesn't matter. Once they get one unnatural movement from the bait, you're done.

In sight fishing, you definitely will not catch every fish you see. In fact, you'll catch a very small percentage of them. But, a lot of times, that small percentage makes for a really big string.

Depending on what you're used to, sight fishing can demand a serious mental adjustment. Once I was fishing with Rick Clunn and we were seeing schools of fish. And, we were catching some and having a good time. When you look back on the day, it was a good one. But, Rick didn't like it because he was seeing all of these fish and he's seeing how many he couldn't catch.

Assuming there is no wind, if I can see the fish flare his gills and suck the bait in, once that bait is gone, to me, it's over... I've got him.

Sometimes, the fish will suck it in and blow it out so fast, you just can't believe it. Other times, the fish get antsy and just pick it up by the tail. I've had a fish pick the tube up by the tail and the hook is laying outside his mouth. You know there's nothing you can do except let him swim off and spit it out. Most of these odd strikes come during the spawn.

Every fish is different. They're all individuals. You'll work a fish and from his fin movements and attitude, you can tell he is aggressive. You say to yourself "I can catch this fish." The next one you throw to may have a very different attitude like "Who cares?" Minute by minute, you'll change from different fish and different attitudes.

Look for active fin movement and for those fish who stay away from the bait then suddenly turn towards it. Those are the ones to start working hard.

Before I developed my High Performance (HP) Kahle hook with a baitholding clip, I used an exposed hook and 1/16-ounce head. As a result. I always had to swim and float the tube bait instead of pitching it. Now, with the HP hook, I've not only

Shaw Grigsby on Sight Fishing continued

improved my catch ratio, but I can fish in heavy cover with any size line or sinker.

When you first hook big Florida bass, it's like they want to deny there is anything wrong. They sit there for a second, shake their head once or twice. Then it's like they say "Forget it, I'm outta here!". It may only be a hesitation of a half second. To me, it seems like a long time. It takes the fish that little bit of time to get spooked. Then, they book it.

> *I feel that backreeling adds a degree of control*
> *you need to be truly successful in finesse fishing.*

While I'm a firm believer in drags on everything, especially sight fishing with spinning reels, I feel that backreeling adds a degree of control you need to be truly successful in finesse fishing. I always keep the drag loose. Whether I'm fishing 6 or 8-pound test, it's loose enough that I can pull line off my reel without wrapping it around my hand. So, when I set the hook, the drag will give a little. That just tells me if anything gets out of control, the drag is going to give and I'll be okay.

When fishermen get a bass to the boat, many let go of the handle and a lot of bad things start happening. To keep the spool from spinning backwards, I hold my middle and ring fingers (on my reel hand) against the bail roller knob. This allows me to control the rod and reel with one hand while providing one last fail-safe mechanism to give line should a fish make one last surge. This is especially important when dealing with smallmouths who are notorious for that one last run.

After winning the 1984 Red Man All-American, Shaw Grigsby launched a career on the B.A.S.S.® circuit and has become one of America's top bass fishing professionals. Much of his success including two Texas Invitational wins in 1988 and 1990 were due to his mastery of sight fishing techniques.

In his own words ... Guido Hibdon on Tubes in Current

Whenever you have a real heavy current, many fishermen make the mistake of sizing up to a heavier jig or slip sinker. I still use the little bitty stuff.

In swift water, you may have to cast at a different angle to put your bait on target. It's like the fly fisherman who casts upstream and lets his fly float past the fish.

After all, fish in current are not used to seeing a baitfish that falls past them quickly. On the James and Potomac rivers, I use 1/8 or 1/4-ounce jigs all the time. Everybody else seems to use 1/2 or 3/4-ounce jigs whenever they get in heavy current.

You have to visualize what a baitfish would look like to a bass going past that piece of structure instead of worrying about putting the bait on his head. To begin with, these fish don't move that fast in current. You have to "filter" the bait to the fish.

In windy conditions, the problem is similar, but you have to position your boat much differently. If you're using light stuff, you have to get the boat upwind of the fish and use the breeze to your advantage.

Basically, I use three rigs for fishing the G2 tube bait: The first is the open hook jig head which is especially useful for skipping under docks. The second is the very same jighead, but rigged with 4 or 5 strands of clear weedguard. And, the third is the Texas-rig with Shaw Grigsby's High Performance hook.

First off, many people don't believe that little baits will catch big fish, but they do. Gosh, we've proven it for years. And, for years before that the guys out west were proving it.

Second, fishermen tend to use too much weight. And, with too much weight the baits don't work right.

With a BassMaster Classic® win in 1988 and back-to-back Angler of the Year titles in '90 and '91, Guido Hibdon dispelled the myth that finesse tactics do not catch big bass and could not win tournaments.

Grubs

Rebirth of the Grub

For years, the grub performed yeoman's work in virtual ano-nymity. Viewed more as a specialty lure or a spinnerbait trailer, the grub always took a backseat to the venerable plastic worm. If you were to compare plastic baits to automobiles, the grub was that 10-year-old pickup truck that always started, but never was driven into town on Saturday night.

Until a few years ago, the grub was a lure in exile. Once the darling of the tournament circuit in the hands of such fabled bassers as Bobby Murray, grubs became the forgotten bait, except for those rare occasions and special applications when they could again prove their worth.

Then, a curious sequence of events occurred which tipped the bass fishing landscape towards the plastic grub. First, bass fishermen discovered the value of taste and scent in plastic baits, a movement originally stimulated by salt-impregnated lures and pushed along by fish-attracting scents. Science was making its presence known in bass fishing and the more we learned, the more we wanted to incorporate this new-found advantage in the baits we used.

The rebirth of interest in grubs has its roots in the West where interest in the curlytail Twin T grub spurred Arizona lure-maker, Gary Yamamoto to add the bait to his lineup - a line that already included Yamamoto's own single-tail, skirted Hula Grub.

At the same time, the salt-and-pepper color phenomenon was gripping the southwest more firmly than a Hulk Hogan hammerlock. Already enamored with the salt-and-pepper colors, it was an easy step for bass fishermen to include salt-and-pepper grubs to their arsenals.

Grub continued

While Yamamoto was the first to reap rewards from this re-kindled interest in grubs, another luremaker - Al Kalin from Brawley, California - joined the fray. Having competed in numerous tournaments on clear-water, western impoundments, Kalin was one of the first to recognize the approaching tide of the finesse revolution. Crucial to the design of his grubs and their subsequent success was Kalin's belief in maximum action at ultra-slow speeds - a tenet that has become the very underpinnings of finesse fishing.

Using the Kalin grub in winning the 1987 U.S. Open at Lake Mead, veteran tourney pro, Larry Hopper, credits the improved tail action of modern grubs for their renewed popularity.

"Grubs these days are more lifelike and resemble the baitfish bass feed on, like shad or bluegill. With smoke and salt-and-pepper colors and various colored flakes, the grubs really look like the baitfish," says Hopper. "I haven't figured it all out, but there are definite times when the bass will take a grub a lot better than they will a plastic worm."

"Unless you put it on a heavy head, the grub is a very light, slow-falling bait. And, with the swimming tail, it has a different action."

According to Kalin, "The discovery of the grub's effectiveness and versatility was made by a lot of average fishermen who listened to the bass fishing grapevine. It was a word-of-mouth, grass-roots situation in which the pros learned about the grub right along with everyone else."

A good deal of the grub's new-found popularity is the result of its undeniable versatility in both finesse and conventional applications. For the finesse fisherman, the grub is well-suited for a variety of techniques and, when the light-line angler puts down the spinning rod for a flippin' stick, the grub is one finesse bait that crosses over without missing a beat.

Finesse Flippin' -- Gary Klein

Known as a fisherman who builds on his strengths, pro basser Gary Klein is one who has discovered an important niche for the grub in his flippin' and pitchin' arsenal.

"Since I'm basically a shallow-water fisherman, I've just taken these grubs and applied them to the same methods I've always used. And I seem to get a few more strikes with them, especially if I'm fishing behind someone or I'm in an area with heavy fishing pressure."

To Klein, the keys are getting the grub to fall vertically near a target and keeping the bait's movement fairly simple.

Rigged on his usual 17- or 20-pound test line (Klein occasionally drops down to 14-pound test), and fished on a flippin' stick, the grub offers a compact bait that is attractive to finicky bass affected by cold fronts, fishing pressure or any combination of adverse factors. Although Klein does use larger 5-inch grubs, he especially likes the 3-inch versions in many situations, particularly when bass become conditioned to larger baits.

Equally important to Klein is the presentation of the grub. To him, the keys are getting it to fall vertically near a target and keeping the bait's movement fairly simple. He doesn't shake the bait or do anything fancy with it, but Klein is a stickler for making his first casts count.

"The most crucial time is the entry on the first sink," he says. "That's usually when the fish will hit your grub. If they're really on that bait, chances are you won't even have your reel engaged when you receive the strike. The hits come real quick in shallow water."

Finesse Flippin' -- Ken Cook

Another top professional who has discovered the versatility of grubs is Oklahoma basser, Ken Cook.

"I use Kalin grubs every which way," says Cook. "Depending on the situation, I may rig them on a darter jig with an exposed hook or I may flip or pitch them rigged Texas-style."

When flipping grubs, Cook utilizes one of Gary Klein's Black Weapon hooks, preferring a 5/0 size that puts the hook bend at the narrower "waist" of the grub. By adding a glass bead to his rig (between slip sinker and hook), Cook brings yet another element of finesse fishing to the up-close, in-your-face world of flippin'.

For Cook, the power of the grub showed itself most graphically at the 1988 BassMasters Classic® on the James River near Richmond, Virginia. With only one small fish to weigh the first day, Cook found himself in 36th place and in desperate need of some new tactics. Switching from jigs and plastic worms to 5-inch Kalin grubs, Cook began a breathtaking run at the championship. The next day, Cook brought in five fish weighing 11-10 which vaulted him into 18th place, still well over 6 pounds behind the leader, Woo Daves.

On the final day, Cook's revised methodology (flippin' Kalin grubs off the deeper end of fallen timber) turned up an even bigger limit totalling 14-3, anchored by the largest fish of the Classic®, a 6-0. Although Guido Hibdon won the 1988 Classic®, Ken Cook's amazing third place finish left him just 1 pound and 5 ounces away from victory - leaving the armchair quarterbacks to wonder "What if Cook had started using the grub a day earlier?"

Splitshotting the Grub

Sizing up by using the grub can be an effective way to discourage sub-keepers from striking and encourage larger fish to react. Many times, just the change in profile and action can result in more strikes. However, a move up in bait size also demands a move up in hook size and, quite often, line test.

Although a 5-inch grub can be used for splitshotting, the result is a lure that generally overpowers the rest of the rig. A better choice is a 3-inch grub which can be fished on eight-pound test and rigged on a 2/0 worm hook. With this setup, the 2/0 hook can be "skin hooked" in the grub (the hook point is imbedded just under the skin of the bait, not through the body as in normal Texas rigging) so the hook has less plastic to penetrate on the hookset. The only drawback to this "skin hook" rig is that the hook no longer serves as a true keel along the seam of the bait. As a result, a too-fast retrieve can sometimes cause the bait to roll over.

In most instances, sizing up from six- to eight-pound test is not much of a trade-off and makes for far better hooksets with the larger 2/0 hook.

If you really have a yen for splitshotting the larger, 5-inch grub, you would be better served fishing it on a traditional Carolina rig with a 12-pound test main line connected to an 8-pound leader. The connection between these two is made through a Sampo swivel which acts as a stop for the 1/8- to 1/4-ounce barrel sinker used in this configuration. Again, you would need to skin hook a worm hook with the Carolina rig, preferably with a 3/0 for the 5-inch grub.

Since 5-inch grubs like Kalin's generate so much torque from their tail action, any rig which moves the weight away from the grub has a tendency to produce roll overs. To reduce this twisting action, the retrieve must be slowed accordingly which, in essence, brings the retrieve of a Carolina rig more in line with that of a normal, hop-and-move Texas rig.

Darter Jigging the Grub

Using the weight-forward, exposed-hook darter jig with the seductive tail action and bulky profile of the grub makes for an especially deadly and versatile rig.

Without any plastic to pull through on the hookset, the darter jig delivers some advantages right from the get-go. Then, the slow-fall action of the grub really comes into play.

Whether a grub is being jumped down ledges, moved over grass beds or cast to breaking fish, if it works at slow speeds, it offers some unique, fish-catching opportunities. To enhance its slow-fall presentation, a light darter head (such as a 1/16-ounce model) should be used whenever possible. Bouncing off ledges, the slow-falling chracteristics of this rig keeps the bait in the strike zone longer. Over breaking fish, the slow fall more accurately duplicates a wounded baitfish struggling against the pull of gravity. Or, in a swimming presentation, the reduced sink rate allows the angler to keep the bait in the strike zone without excessive rodwork or reeling.

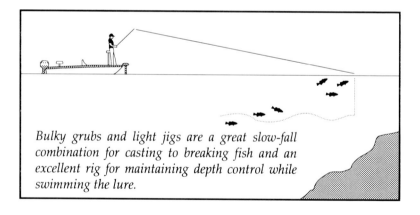

Bulky grubs and light jigs are a great slow-fall combination for casting to breaking fish and an excellent rig for maintaining depth control while swimming the lure.

Deep Water Grubbing

Depending on wind and current conditions, fishing the grub in deep water usually demands heavier jig heads, whether they be darters, football heads or some other style - not only to get down fast, but to maintain more direct contact with the angler. While every different situation involves a certain degree of creativity, there are some basic rules of thumb in fishing grubs deep:

• In most retrieves, you need to lift and move the grub more deliberately than one would a doodle or weenie worm. The shaking motion normally associated with darter jigging or doodling tends to hook the broad grub tail over the hook point of the jig.

• With heavier jigs in the 3/4 to one-ounce range, the grub is often moved across structure by either drifting with a light wind or by moving the boat with the trolling motor.

• The ability to pinpoint fish-holding areas is very important. The ability to put a bait on target is equally important. What often separates the struggling deep-water fisherman from the truly successful one is in the ability to not only evaluate an area, but to put a bait on target at great depths.

If the fish are scattered across main lake flats or a large, flat point, the drift technique demands less specific targeting, but a solid, general knowledge of where the fish are located.

• Often, deep-water bass will only strike a very slow-moving bait and one that does not force them to move very far.

Deep Water Grubbing -- Larry Hopper

• As the weather warms in summer, the gliding action of a darter head can help in keeping the bait in the strike zone longer. This is especially effective along steep walls. According to western deep-water expert, Larry Hopper, this situation is one that demands a slow fall through the strike zone.

"I'll cast parallel to the wall as possible and, for the first part of the cast, I'll peel off line to give the grub a vertical fall and get it down to the strike zone in deep water as quickly as possible. Then, I put the reel in gear and let the bait swing back along the wall through the strike zone."

To insure a straight fall down the cliff wall Larry Hopper peels off line by hand. Once the bait reaches the strike zone, he lets the bait swing back along the wall.

As Hopper strips off line, he keeps a close eye out for strikes on the fall. In this case, hits usually comes as nothing more than a tightening of the line. Even at depths of 30 feet or more, strikes often have the classic "wet rag", pressure-bite feel, says Hopper. As a result, he places a good deal of emphasis on properly sharpened hooks and effective hooksets.

However, on the hookset issue, Hopper goes against what may be the norm by opting for shorter, 5'9" baitcasting rods.

"A lot of people like the long rods, but a shorter one gives me better control. When I set the hook, I reel down and pull up with a short jerk, not a long, sweeping action. I really don't have any problem getting the hook into the fish," he says.

The Grub as Buzzbait

One of the little known, but highly effective uses of the grub is its ability to double as a topwater bait. Rigged on a 3/0 or 4/0 Mister Twister Keeper hook without a slip sinker, the grub can be cast accurately with conventional, baitcasting tackle and simply retrieved quickly across the surface. With the rodtip held in a relatively high position during the retrieve to keep the grub gurgling along the surface, the turbulent action of grubs, like Kalin's 7-inch Mogambo, produce a decidedly subtle, buzzbait-type action.

This finesse application of the grub is particularly effective in shallow, clear water where the bass could be easily spooked by a conventional buzzbait. An additional advantage of the buzzbait grub comes when bass either short-strike or miss the bait completely. With the grub, the retrieve can be stopped following the missed strike, allowing the grub to fall like an injured baitfish. Unlike a conventional buzzbait, the grub does not lose its effectiveness once the retrieve is stopped. Instead, an angler can keep the grub in the strike zone for a follow-up hit.

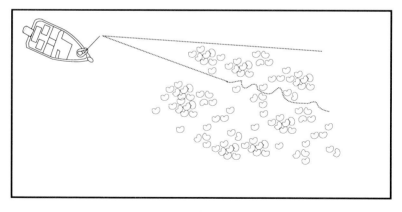

Whether it's a straight, buzzbait-type retrieve or a buzz-and-stop method that allows the grub to drop into the pockets, the grub as buzzbait adds subtlety and versatility to your topwater attack.

In his own words ... Greg Hines on Swimming the Grub

Many times, I fish grubs on the fall. I'll make my casts along walls or cliffs, fishing parallel and let it fall on light line. On 6- or 8-pound test line, the grub has a slow fall and anytime the bait stops, a fish has got it.

After I catch a few fish this way, I'll have a pretty good idea at what depth the fish are hitting. Or, if I find a solid thermocline or get a strong baitfish reading at a certain depth, I'll try to swim the bait along in that zone.

On lakes like Mead and Mohave, sometimes I'll pull my boat in right next to the cliff, put my rodtip close to the wall and just move the bait with my trolling motor. At times, I'll swim it in a nice, easy pumping motion. Other times, I'll just shake it all the way.

Normally, the strikes are very subtle because they don't have to run out from anywhere, you're right there with them. You'll be moving the bait and all of a sudden, it just stops. If you lift the rod just a little, you can feel the fish. Then, it's important to simply reel for all you're worth. Don't worry about the big hookset. You just want that rod flexed when he releases his grip to set the hook.

When you're working the bait, you'll want to keep a constant tension against it. Not tight, but solid contact with the lure. When the fish takes the bait, the line seems to tighten for a second, then releases. If you didn't pull on that, you missed a fish.

In open, clear water situations, you have to be careful not to force the fish to the surface. Once a fish grabs the bait, they pull on it and move. When they realize they're hooked, they start running. If you pull them and get them headed to the top, they'll run to the top.

It's better to pull into them, load your rod and get good rod flex. Of course, you have to use the right action rod which, to me, is a softer action medium to medium light. Just load into the fish. In a split second, the fish will get his head and take off. Once he

Greg Hines on Swimming the Grub continued

does that, you've got him. He's released his grip, he's scared, he's swimming. And, he's going away from you which helps set the hook.

If you pull hard on the fish and get him coming to the top, he'll start shaking his head coming up. Many times the hook is never in the fish and comes out on the way up. Or, he'll run all the way to the top, you'll never get a good pull on him and he'll jump.

To evaluate cliff walls, look for bends in the river channel. If you have a vertical wall where the main river channel or creek channel comes against and makes a bend, that is a key spot. The shad will migrate along that channel and pile up against those corners. Whether it is the main river channel with outside cliffs or in the back of a cove where the creek channel bends, this is the key to finding productive cliff walls.

At more dramatic places like Lake Powell where the cliffs go down 400 to 500-feet under water, I try to fish shelfs on the cliffs. I try to find a shelf - which may be only two to three feet long - at the depth where the fish are holding.

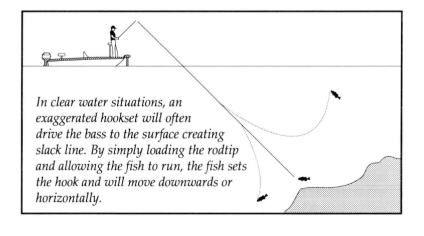

In clear water situations, an exaggerated hookset will often drive the bass to the surface creating slack line. By simply loading the rodtip and allowing the fish to run, the fish sets the hook and will move downwards or horizontally.

Arizona pro Greg Hines has been a top pro wherever he has competed including a 1981 U.S. Open win and two Classic® appearances.

In his own words ... Joe Thomas on Grubs in the Grass

When fishing grass beds less than 15 feet deep, I normally use a 5-inch Kalin grub, a 1/8-ounce sinker, a 4/0 hook and 10-pound test line unless the water is a little dingy, then I'll go to 12-pound test.

This is a good high-pressure system type of bait. When it's cloudy and overcast, grassbed fish will eat anything; a big, slow-rolled spinnerbait, a Rat-L-Trap across the top. But, when a high-pressure situation rolls through, they really lock down and you've got to finesse them out of the grass.

The best way to do this is to slow down with the grub and a light sinker. Just swim it through the tops of short, emergent vegetation (grass less than three feet tall) and tick the top, popping it out, letting it fall, popping it out - just a slow, swimming motion. The 1/8-ounce sinker will not let the grub fall down inside the grass and get lost.

In most cases, the tops of the grass will be somewhere between five and fifteen feet below the surface. I use baitcasting tackle, specifically a 6 to 6 1/2-foot, medium action rod.

When these high-pressure systems move through, I've found that the bass lock on the edges of the grass line. They'll be very non-aggressive, but will hold right on the edge where the grass breaks off to a clean bottom. If you can get the grub to swim along the edge of the grass, you can usually get them to come out after it. But, you need something very slow and subtle because the fish will not go after an outrageous bait like a spinnerbait. The bass just raise their head up and *zip*, they've got it.

The grub has to contact the grass fairly often. Swim it through and shake your rodtip. The key, however, is that clean edge. If you're fishing a pocket with scattered grass or clumps of grass, you can't hone in on the fish. This is what makes this tactic a true finesse technique. You have to use your locator, stay on the edge of the grass line and make short, 45-degree angle pitches (20 to 25 feet) in front of the boat.

Hand line the bait out until it hits the grass, then swim it at a 45-

Joe Thomas on Grubs in the Grass continued

degree angle across the edge of the grass line. Obviously, this keeps the bait in the strike zone longer and keeps you on top of the edge. This 45-degree tactic has proven to be more effective than parallel casting along the edge because the bass are generally right on the edge or three to five feet back in the grass.

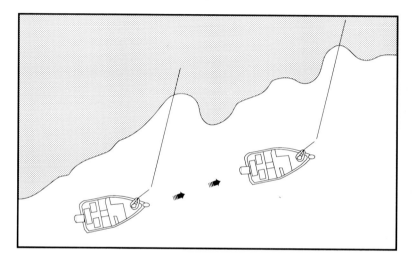

Joe Thomas prefers working grass lines with 45-degree casts to irregularities along the edge. Casts are made 3 to 5 feet back in the grass and brought out. The boat is positioned along the edge of the grassline.

If the grass bed is located on the edge of a river channel, there will be a break to deeper water. But, this is not always the case. At a lake like Okeechobee, there are no dropoffs, the grass bed just stops growing because of a change in bottom composition.

An important key to making this technique effective is finding a small point, pocket or other irregularity in the grass line. This is where the bass pile up.

Joe Thomas knows grubs having won the 1990 Red Man All American championship with that lure. Joe has also become a consistent pro on the B.A.S.S.® circuit having qualified for three Classics®.

Electronics

Mastering the Moment

In more hazardous sports like hang gliding or mountain climbing, the consequences of a serious mistake force you to keep your ego under control. In other words, you have to know precisely how good and how experienced you are when faced with any new situation.

Such self-imposed honesty could go a long way in the bass fishing fraternity, particularly when it comes to fishing electronics. Although thousands of anglers spend millions of dollars each year on electronics, many fishermen have a tough time admitting that they're deficient either in operating their units or evaluating the information or both.

The following chapter gives you a very simple, step-by step means of progressing from novice to intermediate to advanced electronics user. Or, it can simply be used as a refresher course during those inevitable slumps when the fish just won't cooperate.

In finesse fishing, especially vertical applications such as darter jigging and doodling, a strong, working knowledge of your electronics is imperative. Without it, you might as well be wearing handcuffs and a blindfold. In vertical finesse applications, particularly in deep water, YOU MUST MASTER YOUR ELECTRONICS.

Applying the Technology

In the past few years, fishing sonar has become increasingly easier to operate. Unfortunately, the human counterpart of the fish-finding equation often makes the process more difficult than it need be. Quite frankly, there is a point where one must recognize that a mind full of fishing knowledge is not worth much unless that information can be refined, focused and applied on the water.

While speed in locating fish is obviously more critical to the tournament angler, every recreational fisherman, like it or not, is also on a fairly tight schedule. In fact, the weekender who annually spends less time on the water needs to pay greater attention to time management than the tourney angler who has the opportunity to pre-fish waters before the actual tournament days.

But, what's the answer? How does someone wade through the seemingly endless maze of seasonal patterns, weather, temperature, pH, water clarity, baitfish movements, thermoclines, et cetera, et cetera? How do you simplify the use of fishing electronics without reducing their effectiveness?

First, you must recognize that every angler goes through an "evolution" with his or her electronics - from simply finding structure to evaluating cover on that structure to accurately and precisely locating fish.

In this progression from novice to advanced, a fisherman needs to use the knowledge gained to make the process of finding fish less, not more difficult. From novice to intermediate to advanced, the following program offers some very straightforward tactics to help speed and simplify the use of fishing electronics. Although fishermen more experienced in the use of their electronics may want to skim over the more basic techniques, this three-tiered program keeps things in clear perspective regardless of one's skill level. On tough days, you can start from level one and take a quick refresher course. When the fish are cooperating, less advanced electronic anglers can move up the ladder to begin refining their techniques.

Level 1

For someone just getting acquainted with their electronics, you must narrow the search down to the absolute basics: **Find activity at <u>any</u> depth**.

The key, however, is not to simply look for fish activity, but for a complete array of activity from the top to the bottom of the food chain.

If you do not see any marks near the surface, any widening of the zero line that would indicate bait activity or algae / plankton (the eco chain for the fish), then consider this analogy: If nobody is home, if the house is vacant, why sit there and wait for the homeowner to show up?

When the picture is clean, you can feel confident you're in sterile water. Sonar units don't generate false echoes nor do they produce images from nothing. Unfortunately, too many fishermen try to produce fish where there are none.

Of course, the toughest decision for any angler is where to start the search. But, even this common dilemma can be handled rather easily.

First, break the lake down into major habitat areas (i.e. creek channels, points, flats, steep banks, etc.) and look for activity in those major areas.

Level 1 continued

For example, any major creek or tributary is going to be a prime habitat area. These locations generally offers bass just about everything they need. From deep-water sanctuary to spawning areas to sunny banks to shady banks to windward banks to leeward banks to ledges to humps to flats.

Within such a diverse area, an activity zone will show up very clearly on an liquid crystal screen or paper graph with a variety of marks denoting fish, bait and everything in between. In this search, you're not looking for something subtle. Rather, it is finding a flurry of activity that identifies the best opportunities for success. Similarly, you are not looking for fish arches at a specific depth or in a specific location within the chosen search area. The idea is simply to look for general, overall activity. This puts you in the ballpark. Then, expand your search in that area to locate fish arches.

After one such activity area has been located and fished, the next step is to check out portions of the lake that offer both *matching* and *different* structure and cover. By doing so, you will be able to see if the presence of activity and fish is dependent on certain conditions being present.

If you want to take this simple procedure one step further, you can break the lake down in even broader terms. For example, a fisherman can begin the search merely by comparing the difference between windy areas as opposed to protected areas. Is the greatest activity on the windward side of a point or on the leeward side?

You can also cut down the search time by taking current fishing information offered by others and use your electronics to determine if it is worthwhile. Although "dock talk" can often hinder your fishing more than help it, you can quickly validate the hearsay with your electronics. If it proves to be accurate, buy that man a cold one. If it proves to be false, you have wasted little time and eliminated one possibility from the daily puzzle.

Level 1 - Summary

Whatever criteria is used, the procedure remains the same:

- Break the lake down into general areas.

- Find activity that shows a full spectrum of life from baitfish to gamefish at any depth.

- Check similar and dissimilar areas to confirm what you've found.

- Don't waste time fishing "sterile" water.

- Use your electronics to validate fishing information.

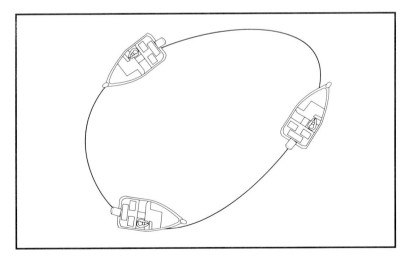

To get a more complete look at structure, use an oval search pattern rather than taking straight passes across the area.

Level 2

At the intermediate level, a fisherman should begin focusing his or her efforts in a specific depth range by utilizing the information provided by one's electronics. Now, it is a matter of "fine tuning" the specifics.

To do this, the advice is simple as it is effective: When motoring out of the marina at the start of a day's fishing, turn on your liquid crystal or paper graph and find the specific depth range where the greatest activity is present. Even if the activity should appear at 20 feet over water that is much deeper, the activity zone will usually be found consistently at that depth throughout the rest of the lake.

Then, the object is to focus your attention and efforts around key structure in that productive depth range. By narrowing the area of focus, an intermediate fisherman can maximize his or her fishing time quite effectively.

Should the activity zone be spread over a fairly broad depth range, then it is a matter of keying on that depth which best suits your fishing style. Obviously, a fisherman skilled in deep-water tactics would probably opt for those fish in 20 to 30 feet over those found in 5 to 10 feet. The point is simply maximizing your strengths or, in more succinct terms, "Throw what you know."

On the other hand, it is a fool who tries to make something out of nothing. As previously stated in Level 1, the key is fishing in obvious activity areas and not in trying to pull fish from "sterile" water. By focusing on the very best areas that offer the very best chances for success, you will be spending less time trying to evaluate your electronics and more time catching fish.

In those situations where no overt activity zone shows up on the graph, all is not lost since electronics also tell you where they're not. And, if there are no signs of life in deep or shallow water, it is probably a safe assumption that the fish have sucked up tight into cover.

Level 2 - Summary

The intermediate level is generally where fishermen get overwhelmed by the electronic power at their disposal. Instead of simplifying the procedure, far too many anglers actually go out of their way to complicate it. To avoid this pitfall, remember:

> • Focus on the specific depth level where the activity is present.

> • Throw what you know.

> • Don't try to make something happen. Prime areas are very obvious and show great activity with baitfish present and fish positioned in a variety of ways over, in or around cover and structure. Focus on those key zones.

> • Your electronics also tell you where the fish *are not* located. Use this knowledge to your best advantage.

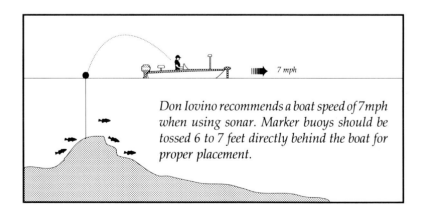

Don Iovino recommends a boat speed of 7 mph when using sonar. Marker buoys should be tossed 6 to 7 feet directly behind the boat for proper placement.

Level 3

As you have seen in Levels 1 and 2, the simplification process in the use of fishing electronics is gradually narrowing the search area as one's skill improves. Levels 1 and 2 ask the fisherman to "focus" on a specific depth range within a general activity zone. In Level 3, you narrow the "target" area. Now, it becomes a matter of "pinpointing" a specific part of the structure at the chosen depth level which has the greatest probability of holding fish.

The ability to quickly find the area of greatest probability is often what separates those who consistently catch fish from those who do not. And, it separates those who can find fish in unfamiliar lakes or under adverse weather conditions from those who cannot.

How many times have you seen fishermen run back and forth over an area, drop 4 or 5 marker buoys to map it out and end up using more time to mark a spot than they will to fish it? Not to mention they cause so much commotion in the process, the bass are twice as wary as usual.

The ability to quickly find the area of greatest probability is often what separates those who consistently catch fish from those who do not.

Clearly, the best approach is to move in, find the highest point or steepest break on a piece of structure and hit it. That is the area of greatest probability. It's got the best ambush point, it's got the quickest and best deep-water access. If there are no fish on the best area of the structure, then why work the structure out? If there is not even a straggler on the best contact point, chances are the group of fish that normally hang out or use that area are suspended. But, if you catch some fish, expand your search. The fish may be moving or there may be several more fish on ambush in and around that area.

Level 3 continued

In many ways, this tactic is comparable to methods used when casting to visible structure where a skilled angler casts first to the most likely fish-holding section of a laydown tree, dock or brushpile. If this "best offering" doesn't draw any interest and a fisherman is trying to maximize his or her fishing time, little effort is wasted on longshot presentations. However, should a key portion of the cover turn up a fish, then a more detailed investigation is in order.

Extreme focus is the manner in which a fisherman experienced in the use of electronics can reduce the search time and cover more water in the process. By pinpointing the key area within an area and by having the confidence to believe in one's fishing talent, an angler can evaluate a larger piece of structure by what happens in a small section.

Level 3 - Summary

To make things simple for advanced operation:

- Resist the temptation to graph every inch of a fishing location.

- Find the best area within an area that offers the greatest potential for success.

- When fish are caught expand your search area. If not, move on to the next general area, find the key spot there and repeat the process.

Although the incredible array of high-tech fishing products might indicate otherwise, the most successful fishermen are generally those who can break down any situation into its most basic parts. Given the chance, your electronics can help you do just that.

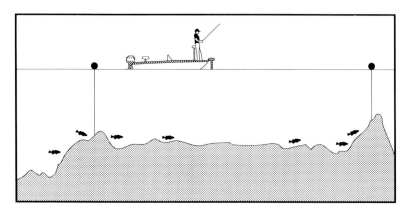

To help visualize deeper structure and provide visual reference points, drop a marker buoy at each end of a ridge, hump or rockpile. Then, try to create a mental image of the area being fished.

In his own words ... Don Siefert on Finesse Electronics

Finesse fishing is largely associated with deep, clear lakes and marginal cover. Electronics can and do play a major role in the focus of your presentation or pattern.

Unlike the long casts used to cover large areas with heavy, bottom-bouncing lures, finesse fishing relies on subtle, life-like baits with line tests down into the four-pound test range. As a result, the optimum presentation of any finesse bait or method is, to some degree, restricted to a smaller radius from the boat. Not to mention that boat position and movement, either by electric motor or drift, also has a tremendous bearing on how effective your efforts will be.

We must look deeper into our electronics than just the detection of obvious structure. Just as finesse fishing is a refinement of other methods, we must also refine the role of our electronics. Instead of merely reading the bottom signal of our flasher, liquid crystal or chart recorder, we need to study the second echo. This shows bottom composition changes, weed lines, moss, ditches and holes, individual large boulders, road beds and foundations, just to name a few.

Another critical item is transducer placement and angle. This allows us to know exactly where these targets are located and how to effectively address them. From vertical doodling to drifting with a splitshot, you can remove the guesswork.

What do you want to look for? In the second echo, think of two circles, a larger one with a smaller one directly in the center. Everything in the larger circle shows up as your first echo. The second echo is simply the second bounce of your sonar signal. Since various things absorb the sonar energy, the second echo only displays the strongest return signals. Road beds or flat rocks are classic examples.

For instance, as you come over a road bed, the second echo will increase in intensity. If you've tuned your sonar so you barely get a second echo over sand, then whenever you change composition such as a muddy bottom, the second echo will disappear. If you go over a harder bottom like a road bed, foundation

Don Siefert on Finesse Electronics continued

or flat rock, the second echo will intensify and, in many cases, become very defined.

Adjusting your second echo is very simple. Keep this in mind: They never build a launch ramp on mud. Nor do they pick muddy areas for swim beaches. Use these areas to adjust your second echo to barely register on a sandy bottom.

Remember, the depth is the first echo. The second echo tells you the nature of the object. Also, with a properly tuned second echo, depth changes are more noticeable. A small hole or ditch may go undetected in the primary signal, but if you watch the second echo, you will see these subtleties.

> *Remember, the depth is the first echo.*
> *The second echo tells you the nature of the object.*

I've often been asked by trout and salmon fishermen, "Why do bass fishermen look down at their electronics and then cast away from the boat?" I think it's a great question.

With a 20-degree transducer, the area covered is approximately one-third of the depth: At 30 feet, a sonar is showing ten feet which is actually a five-foot radius around the transducer. With an 8-degree transducer, much less is shown (nearly one-half less than with a 20-degree transducer). Either way, that's not a lot of area.

A tilted transducer on the trolling motor will allow you to double the survey area and pinpoint targets exactly. However, one word of caution: Only tilt the transducer half of its cone angle, i.e. a 10-degree tilt on a 20-degree transducer and a 4-degree tilt on an 8-degree transducer. Otherwise, your depths will be in error and you won't have a true feeling what you are seeing. By tilting the transducer properly, you can now use the arrow on top of your trolling motor for casting directions! Now, you can cast to the fish, not stand over them.

Don Siefert on Finesse Electronics continued

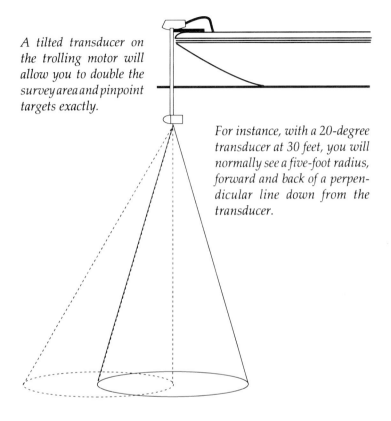

A tilted transducer on the trolling motor will allow you to double the survey area and pinpoint targets exactly.

For instance, with a 20-degree transducer at 30 feet, you will normally see a five-foot radius, forward and back of a perpendicular line down from the transducer.

With a tilted transducer (10 degrees), the search area will be doubled and will be in front of the boat in whatever direction the trolling motor is pointed. This gives you the advantage of seeing structure and fish before you are directly over or past them.

A veteran tournament pro, Don Siefert worked many years developing and marketing fishing electronics. Siefert also conducts instructional seminars on the effective use of electronics and recently completed a video, "Sonar and How to Use It."

Mental

In the preceding pages, you have learned how to expand your mechanical skills to maximize your bass fishing opportunities. This is the intellectual side of things. The following conversation with Rick Clunn explores another important side of fishing performance, the intuitive.

While many have wondered just what makes Rick Clunn so good, few have listened to the real message found in Clunn's phrase "There are no limits." Instead, they choose to focus on the more tangible aspects of his success when, in fact, the intangible is what makes Rick Clunn so special. If you're looking for his "secret," this is it. How (or if) you choose to use this information is up to you.

With four BassMaster Classic® wins, a B.A.S.S. Angler-of-the-Year title, two U. S. Open wins and a Red Man All-American championship to his credit, Rick Clunn has defined the measure of excellence in tournament competition. Yet, for all of his accomplishments in bass fishing, perhaps his most unique insight into fishing success has generated the least amount of publicity.

While fishermen attempt to duplicate Clunn's winning tactics, mechanics and lures, they ignore the most crucial element to his success - Clunn's ability to mentally shut out the external world and tap into his intuitive nature. Instead of allowing negative thoughts to intrude on his performance, Clunn tries to become a part of the natural environment by bringing his intuitive side to the forefront and allowing his intellect to play a complementary or supportive role.

The result of Clunn's mental approach is ultimately something every fisherman has experienced at one time or another. It is that feeling when everything clicks, when you know a fish will strike a moment before it strikes, when it seems as if you're in tune with the elements. At such moments your actions are guided more by powerful subconscious commands that defy normal logic. Why did you cast there? Why did you fish that cove? Not because you intellectually weighed the pros and cons, but simply because you followed your intuitive nature.

Unfortunately, for most people, these moments of heightened awareness are all too brief. Even Clunn, who has been trying to lock into this human potential since 1983, often finds himself unable to reach that level for long periods of time or even to properly react to strong intuitive signals.

One failure for Clunn was at a tournament where he spent a portion of one day (prior to the practice period), relaxing and reading in a park next to the lake. As he sat there, Clunn began to feel the area having a powerful effect on him, yet ignored the signals of what he characterizes as a "strange mechanism." The result? During the tournament, after fishing other areas without great success, Clunn finally acted on his intuitive urgings only to find fellow pro, Jim Bitter, diligently working the area. Bitter won the tournament in that spot. "As much as I work on it," laments Clunn, "I still fail to totally grasp the magnitude of it."

Despite such small setbacks, Clunn obviously has reached this higher level of awareness enough times to set himself apart in a sport where so much seems outside of one's personal control. Perhaps his most dramatic victory came on the James River near Richmond, Virginia where Clunn put his theories to the test at the 1990 Bassmasters Classic®.

"In this Classic®, it was probably the first time I experienced it for the majority of the day. I would say 97 percent of that last day (when Clunn put together an astounding limit to blow past tournament leader Tommy Biffle for his fourth Classic® victory), I experienced that level (of heightened awareness)," remarked Clunn. "That's rarely been the case in the past.

Usually it's been for an hour or maybe two hours."

"Now I'm conscious of it when it happens. Most people are never conscious of it. But, once you're conscious of it, you have the potential of analyzing and understanding what triggers it, what gets you to that level. Then, you start trying to consciously create those situations so you can experience that level of awareness more often."

But, how do you put yourself on that higher level? Will self-help books or positive thinking seminars make a difference? Only if it is part of your personal efforts to pursue this higher understanding of positive thinking, says Clunn, since the problem with books and seminars is in their inability to motivate people over a long period of time.

"A motivational speaker can usually motivate nearly every-one in the audience for "x" amount of time," he observes. "But, the minute they leave, in differing degrees, he starts losing them. Eventually he loses all of them or almost all of them. Perhaps only one percent come out of the meeting and retain it."

At the same time, people have to deal with what Clunn calls a "negatively-dominated" society where even though you may try to maintain positive thoughts for the majority of a day, you're still battling a tremendous amount of negative input from the outside world. So, even if a motivational speaker pumps you up for that one day, there are factors at work pumping you down the other 364 days of the year.

Even the very term "positive thinking" can lend itself to this negativism because the phrase has been misused and over-used to the point where it has no meaning, says Clunn.

So, what's the answer? To Clunn, it means being part of that one percent who take this positive thinking to heart. "It is not something that can be intellectually understood. It has to be something you understand in your heart. Something that takes you past the rhetoric. It's not an easy thing."

"The work is in shutting down what I consider the external world and becoming very internal. Shutting down the man-made world and really getting back to more of a natural state of mind. The intellect is not totally shut out, but it takes on a complementary role, not a dominant role. This is exactly backwards to what society has preached to us - that intellect is all-important. You have to reverse that.

"The intuitive is hardly recognized at all in an intellectual society. It's almost viewed as a weakness. It's very ironic because the intuitive has infinitely more power than intellect, but we don't recognize that in our society. I have to reverse that to where my intuitive is basically the dominant thing and my intellect is serving a complementary role. It's a lot of mental work and discipline.

"For instance, if we could take some of the Apache Indian scouts, who had some of the highest awareness of any people who ever walked the face of the Earth, and apply their awareness abilities to fishing, we would destroy anything we know right now, intellectually-speaking, in tournament fishing.

"Sure, these Indians had intellectual abilities. In other words, how to make bows and arrows and things like that. But, those were just very mechanical things. The real part of their survival had to do with their ultimate awareness of their environment which you can put into the intuitive level. Thank goodness, there are no Indians fishing tournaments."

To Clunn, if you don't allow the intuitive to get involved, intellectual knowledge is simply "a tool without a craftsman to use it." Unfortunately, this is precisely the way most people think, says Clunn. "We think the intellect is the craftsman. It's not, it's only the tool. We basically have a tool with no one to use it."

"The hardest thing in fishing is putting yourself in the right area. This is where the intuitive is so powerful. The easiest thing is technique. But, then again, there is nothing written in concrete with technique, either. You should always have an open mind about that, too."